— Cultivating the Fruit of the Spirit —

— Yan Newberry —

Cultivating the Fruit of the Spirit

NINE FRUITS A DAY

Translated from French by Alison Mowat

Éditions Biblos

Original edition in French, published under the title :
Cultiver le fruit de l'Esprit
par Biblos, France, ISBN : 978-2-912821-12-6

6 ter Av. Teilhard de Chardin – 26700 Pierrelatte – France
ISBN: 978-2-912821-19-5

Typesetting : Éliette Teissier – Excelsis SARL
Illustrations : © Can Stock Photo/Orla et © Can Stock Photo/Kounadeas.
Cover design : Rachel Caro – www.moovima.com

— Contents —

— Acknowledgements —

This book is in your hands because of all of the people who have encouraged me throughout this project. I would like to express my profound gratitude to Éliette Teissier who kindly offered to transfer the recordings of a series of sermons I gave on "Cultivating the fruit of the Spirit" onto the computer. Thank you Éliette for your gifts, and for the precious time which you set aside so that this book might see the light of day.

This book was originally written in French. A big thank you to Alison Mowat who translated this book into Queen's English. Alison's professional touch has enhanced the content and will help the reader cultivate the fruit of the Spirit. Thanks too to Anne and David Speed for the proof reading and helpful suggestions.

I would also like to thank Rachel Caro, our graphic designer, who created a beautiful cover. Last but not least, I extend my thanks to the members of Editions Biblos who have supported the project from start to finish.

I am grateful that the Lord has placed along my path Christians who can cultivate and demonstrate the fruit of the Spirit. Writing these lines, I can put one or more faces to each fruit: love, joy, peace, patience, kindness, goodness, faithfulness, gentleness, self-control. Perhaps you are one of them…

I also salute the hundreds of "silent soldiers" in my library who have made themselves available and helped me to develop and enrich this work.

Who am I to speak of the fruit of the Spirit? Whilst studying this subject, the Holy Spirit has shown me the fruits which I need to work on. Which ones? All nine!

At the end of each chapter, you will find questions to help you get to grips with the themes as an individual or group.

For those who read these lines, I pray that you may feel the presence of the Lord's Spirit and know his power in your everyday life, so that you may cultivate the fruit of the Spirit for yourself and spread them all around you.

— Abbreviations —

Books of the Bible

The Old Testament		The New Testament	
Genesis	Ge	*Matthew*	Mt
Exodus	Ex	*Mark*	Mk
Leviticus	Lev	*Luke*	Lk
Numbers	Nu	*John*	Jn
Deuteronomy	Dt	*Acts*	Ac
Joshua	Jos	*Romans*	Ro
Judges	Jdg	*1 Corinthians*	1Co
Ruth	Ru	*2 Corinthians*	2Co
1 Samuel	1Sa	*Galatians*	Gal
2 Samuel	2Sa	*Ephesians*	Eph
1 Kings	1Ki	*Philippians*	Php
2 Kings	2Ki	*Colossians*	Col
1 Chronicles	1Ch	*1 Thessalonians*	1Th
2 Chronicles	2Ch	*2 Thessalonians*	2Th
Ezra	Ezr	*1 Timothy*	1Ti
Nehemiah	Ne	*2 Timothy*	2Ti
Esther	Est	*Titus*	Tit
Job	Job	*Philemon*	Phm
Psalms	Ps	*Hebrews*	Heb
Proverbs	Pr	*James*	Jas
Ecclesiastes	Ecc	*1 Peter*	1Pe
Song of Songs	SS	*2 Peter*	2Pe
Isaiah	Isa	*1 John*	1Jn

The Old Testament		The New Testament	
Jeremiah	Jer	*2 John*	2Jn
Lamentations	La	*3 John*	3Jn
Ezekiel	Eze	*Jude*	Jude
Daniel	Da	*Revelation*	Rev
Hosea	Hos		
Joel	Joel		
Amos	Am		
Obadiah	Ob		
Jonah	Jnh		
Micah	Mic		
Nahum	Na		
Habakkuk	Hab		
Zephaniah	Zep		
Haggai	Hag		
Zechariah	Zec		
Malachi	Mal		

— Preface —

Nine fruits a day

To keep physically healthy, we are told to eat five fruit and vegetables every day! To remain in shape and have **spiritual energy**, we need to know the fruit of the Spirit, consisting of nine qualities, to have access to its source so that we might cultivate it and, then, to spread it to those around us! What a prospect my friends!

Nothing is simpler than cultivating the fruit of the flesh! All we have to do is let ourselves go: arguments, jealousy, immorality… can very quickly take over our lives. To cultivate the fruit of the Spirit, on the other hand, we have to be attentive to the Holy Spirit and allow His power to manifest itself in our lives. I would like to propose four steps to cultivate the fruit of the Spirit.

Memorise the nine fruits of the Spirit

If you are reading this book, it is surely because you want to cultivate the nine fruits of the Spirit?! Is that right? Do you know them by heart? If that is not the case, open your Bible at Galatians 5:22. The first step is to read this verse several times and memorise the nine fruits listed.

> "But the fruit of the Spirit is love, joy, peace, patience, kindness, goodness, faithfulness, gentleness and self-control. Against such things there is no law" (Galatians 5:22, GNT)

Draw close to God and allow yourself to be transformed by the Holy Spirit

The second step involves asking God to help you access the source of the fruit of the Spirit. This requires profound soul-searching; a desire to draw near to God and to allow yourself to be transformed by the power of the Holy Spirit.

Progress with the help of a "coach"

If we want to make progress in any area of life, we need help and encouragement from an external source. I learnt to play the piano by myself. I had a gift for music and could play almost any piece by ear. But when I decided to get a teacher it changed everything: I realised that I was not using the right fingering or tempo and that my sight-reading was poor. My teacher has helped me to correct so many bad habits and I am now making considerable progress each day. For this third step, choose a coach who will be able to help you cultivate the fruit of the Spirit. It could be a friend, your brother or sister, your husband or wife, someone you know well. They will help you identify your weak and strong points, will encourage you to work on them and pray with you for your progress… Choose a coach!

> *Work purposefully on one fruit each day.*

Make the decision to "radiate" the fruit of the Spirit each day, to live out each fruit where you are, in your family, at work. This will give those around you the desire to know God, the giver of these fruits. As the fourth step, work purposefully on one fruit each day. Today, for example, I am going to focus on "kindness". I will bake a cake for my neighbour, phone or write to a friend… I am sure you have better ideas!

— Introduction —

What ideas does the word "fruit" conjure up in your mind? Growth, fertility, vitality, energy? As the old saying goes, "an apple a day keeps the doctor away". France, where I have lived for many years, exports beautiful fruits to the rest of the world. Throughout the year, the stands at the markets in Provence in particular are swarmed as the fresh produce appears. A large selection of delicious fruits is available to shoppers. And when it is hot in summer, what could be better than a nice melon or a juicy peach? I learnt that the world is home to one hundred and thirty six different types of fruit.

The fruit grown in Scotland, the country I grew up in, does not have the same flavour. When I was a child, a magnificent bowl of fruits took pride of place on the dining room table. A peach, an apple, a grape, a banana would catch my eye. There was only one thing I wanted to do: take them and greedily sink my teeth into them. But I was not allowed to. Why? Because the fruits were made of plastic! The fruit of the Spirit which we are going to discuss in this book is in no way artificial. On the contrary, this fruit is genuine and full of spiritual vitamins!

We are going to contemplate, examine and taste nine different fruits. However, before we look at Galatians 5:22, I would like to give you some insight into the word "fruit" in the Bible.

The different meanings of the word "fruit" in the Bible

In the Old Testament, in the literal sense, it is the edible product of a plant or tree, "the fruit of your ground" (Dt 7:13, English Standard Version). It is interesting to note that during the creation, as highlighted in Genesis 1:11, God injects seeds into the fruits, giving them the capacity to reproduce and multiply. "Let the land produce vegetation: seed-bearing plants and trees on the land that bear fruit with seed in it, according to their various kinds."

In its metaphorical sense, the word "fruit" has several meanings: it can relate to offspring "the fruit of your womb" (Dt 28:11) or the result of an action, such as a reward or salary (Ps 58:11; Pr 31:16).

In the New Testament, the word "fruit" appears fifty-four times, particularly in Matthew's gospel. Its first meaning is as a product of the earth: "See how the farmer waits for the precious fruit of the earth, being patient about it, until it receives the early and the late rains" (Jas 5:7, ESV).

Jesus speaks of fruit as an action or a character trait, the visible expression of an invisible energy from which springs an outcome, good or bad. You can recognise a tree by its fruit. "Likewise, every good tree bears good fruit, but a bad tree bears bad fruit." (Mt 7:17). "A man reaps what he sows." (Gal 6:7).

The Holy Spirit, "invisible agent", lives in the heart of Christians (Jn 14:17). He "grafts" us into Jesus, the true vine. It is the presence and the powerful action of the Holy Spirit which makes us capable of bearing good fruit and lots of it (Jn 15:8).

> The contrast between works and fruit is important. A machine in a factory works, and turns out a product, but it could never manufacture fruit. Fruit must grow out of life, and, in the case of the believer, it is the life of the Spirit (Gal 5.25). When you think of "works" you think of effort, labour, strain, and toil; when you think of "fruit" you think of beauty, quietness, the unfolding of life. The flesh produces "dead works" (Heb 9.14, ESV), but the Spirit produces living fruit. And this fruit has in it the seed for still more fruit (Gen 1.11) (…)" In brief, the secret is the Holy Spirit.[1]

Some texts in the Bible mention other "fruits" which we will not cover in this work: "Produce fruit in keeping with repentance." (Mt 3:8); people won for Christ, "in order that I might have a harvest among you" (Ro 1:13); "for the fruit of the light consists in all goodness, righteousness and truth" (Eph 5:9); "the fruit you reap of being made righteous" (Ro 6:22, J.B. Phillips) and "the fruit of lips that openly profess his name, that is, praise" (Heb 13:15). There are also fruits which follow on from financial donations made to advance God's work, such as those received from the Philippian Church. Paul said: "It isn't the value of the gift that I am keen on, it is the reward that will come to you because of these gifts that you have made" (Php 4:17, J.B. Phillips). Here, Paul compares their gift to a "spiritual investment" for which they will receive eternal interest.

In Greek, the word fruit "karpos" suggests spiritual qualities which spontaneously spring forth from a Christian in whom the Holy Spirit dwells.

Paul's major concern for young Christians was their progress and growth. He prays for the Philippian Church: "And this is my prayer: that your love may abound more and more in knowledge and depth of insight, so that you may be able to discern what is best and may be pure and blameless for the day of Christ, filled with the fruit of righteousness that comes through Jesus Christ—to the glory and praise of God" (Php 1:9-11). To the Christians in Rome, he poses this pertinent question: "But what fruit were you getting at that time from the things of which you are now ashamed?" (Ro 6:21, ESV). He prays that the Colossians will be "bearing fruit in every good work" (Col 1:10). This is a crucial subject for our Churches and one which should be a part of our prayers. Having the fruit of the Spirit in our Churches will attract the attention of others and motivate many of them to become Christians. During my numerous visits to Churches, I could see straightaway that one Church radiated the joy of the Lord, another his kindness and another his peace... Pray that your own Church may bear all the fruits of the Spirit.

Definition: In Greek, the word fruit "karpos" suggests spiritual qualities which spontaneously spring forth from a Christian in whom the Holy Spirit dwells.

Difference between human qualities and spiritual qualities

Man was created in the image of God (Ge 1:26), but this image has been distorted by sin. Natural human qualities are still a part of us but they have deteriorated. The Holy Spirit, when we are born again, will give us and will help us to cultivate spiritual qualities: the fruit of the Spirit.

> Generosity, devotion, friendship and affection can be seen throughout the world. We must celebrate these qualities and not take them for granted; however we should not confuse them with love as it is presented in the Bible. At the furthest limit, Paul believes that it is possible to be so generous that we distribute all our wealth to feed the poor, so devoted as to hand over our body to be burnt and yet still not have love (1Cor 13:3)! To truly experience what God calls on us to feel for Him and our neighbours, we must first open our hearts to God's grace. "We love because he first loved us" (1 Jn 4:19).[2]

A sought-after fruit

Non-Christians seek these fruits today: joy, peace, self-control... And they will turn to any means to acquire them: religion, sport, yoga, music etc.

Difference between the fruit of the Spirit and the gifts of the Spirit

This work does not deal with the gifts of the Spirit but rather the fruit of the Spirit. The two should not be confused. Gifts are for serving others; the fruit of the Spirit is there to change us internally and transform our character. We have a tendency to emphasise the gifts of the Spirit at the expense of the fruit of the Spirit. Yet, to effectively use the gifts of the Spirit, we need the fruit of the Spirit.

> *The fruit of the Spirit is there to change us internally and transform our character.*

A single source

In Galatians 5:22, Paul presents us with a bowl of beautiful fruit: love, joy, peace…

It is worth noting that he speaks of *fruit*, singular, rather than *fruits*.

Why is this? The fruit of the Spirit has a single source: our attachment to Jesus. Jesus reveals the secret to us in John 15:5: "If you remain in me and I in you, you will bear much fruit; apart from me you can do nothing."

These fruits are inseparable

These fruits are linked to one another; they are interdependent, complementary and inseparable. You cannot become a specialist in one fruit. That is not an option; you have to cultivate the nine fruits in the same way. Imagine if you had to eat the same fruit – a banana for example – every day for a week, morning, noon and evening. You would surely grow tired of this and request a more balanced diet! The nine fruits of the Spirit are like the segments of an orange. If you take one segment, you no longer have an orange but orange segments. Each of the fruits, like the segments, are linked to one another. They are part of the same family, share the same DNA and source: the Holy Spirit.

> *These fruits are linked to one another; they are interdependent, complementary and inseparable.*

A question of temperament?

Based on our temperament, we may be able to cultivate some fruits more easily. For example, a placid person knows how to cultivate patience, whereas someone who is quick to anger will have difficulty exercising self-control.

There are Christians who are naturally positive and joyful and it is great to meet such people! Yet these very Christians may perhaps also be easily irritated. Let's prioritise the cultivation of the fruits which we have least of. Personally, I lack patience and gentleness. How about you?

A life choice

Throughout the Bible, we meet men and women who have been able to cultivate good fruits. Joseph, for example, met his brothers' hatred with love and, in this way, "touched their hearts" (Ge 50:21, GNT).

The book of Kings tells the stories of good and bad monarchs. Some chose integrity, faithfulness to God and peace, whereas others preferred pride, rivalries and wars. Josiah chose the first of these two paths: "He did what was right in the eyes of the LORD and followed completely the ways of his father David, not turning aside to the right or to the left" (2Ki 22:2); whereas as Manasseh chose the latter: "He did evil in the eyes of the LORD, following the detestable practices of the nations the LORD had driven out before the Israelites" (2Ki 21:2).

The beautiful city of Jerusalem – described as the holy city (Neh 11:1), the perfection of beauty (La 2:15), a crown of splendour in the Lord's hand (Isa 62:3) – is pillaged and becomes a ghost city, "in great trouble and disgrace. The wall of Jerusalem is broken down, and its gates have been burned with fire" (Ne 1:3). "Surely these things happened to Judah according to the LORD's command, because of the sins of Manasseh" (2Ki 24:3), sins of idolatry, occultism (2Ki 21:1-11).

Notice that making the wrong choice has, sooner or later, harmful repercussions on those around us and future generations.

"Do not be deceived: God cannot be mocked. A man reaps what he sows" (Gal 6:7).

Bearing fruit, one of Jesus' concerns

On several occasions, Jesus speaks of trees or plants which bear (or do not bear) fruit.

He tells the parable of a fig tree which has not borne fruit for three years. This was unusual as fig trees normally bear fruit several times a year (Lk 13:6-9). In the parable, the man who maintains the vineyard suggests fertilising the tree and leaving it for another year. If, after this time, there is still no fruit, the tree will be cut down.

Later, a week before his death, Jesus sees a fig tree without any fruit on his way to Jerusalem. He declares that the tree will never bear fruit and it suddenly withers (Mt 21:19). This is one of the rare destructive miracles performed by Jesus.

These two examples of sterile fig trees and the attitude and action of Jesus should make us think.

In John 15, Jesus uses the image of the vine and its branches to demonstrate that there are three kinds of people:

- Those who *do not* bear fruit: v.2
- Those who bear *more* fruit: v.2
- Those who bear *lots of* fruit: v.5,8

Which category are you in?

A testimony

What I find most encouraging in my Christian life is to see Christians who know how to cultivate and spread the fruit of the Spirit. They radiate love, peace, joy, etc. and it is not dependant on circumstances. They make you want to be like them!

We know an elderly Christian in Nice who rents out the ground floor of her house in the summer. This friend is filled with the love of God and, without even speaking, she communicates this to those around her. One summer, when saying goodbye to one of her lodgers, she said “God Bless you”. The testimony which she gave just through the way she lives her life and these few words had such a remarkable impression on this tourist that, once she was home, she phoned our friend to ask her why she was different from everyone she had ever met. To this, our friend was able to say that she had God in her life. This lady then went on to become a Christian. What a beautiful testimony! We must let the love of God express itself through us; let it flow abundantly so that other hearts may be touched and transformed.

— Introduction to Galatians 5:22 —

In order to make sense of this verse, we need to understand the context in which it is written. The insight gained from meeting a Scotsman wearing a kilt in the highlands is not the same as meeting this same Scotsman in the Sahara desert. The cultural, historical and geographical settings are essential to understand his context.

In the same way, when we read a passage from the Bible, we need to be aware of its context. By understanding the culture and environment from which a passage arises, we can appreciate it and the spiritual nourishment it provides us with.

In this study, we want to know the context of the verse and understand why Paul speaks about the fruit of the Spirit. The apostle is writing to several Churches in a large region. Paul visits this region as a missionary during several different trips – details in Acts 13:49; 14:8-21; 16:6; 17-23. The cities of Iconia, Derbe and Lystra were all part of Galatia, now Turkey.

Paul writes to these Churches for four reasons…

They had turned away from the Gospel (1:6)

After Pauls' visits, these Churches were visited by Jewish preachers who called on them to return to the Law of Moses and contested the Good News announced by the apostle. The Christians gradually allowed themselves to be weighed down by the yoke of legalism and forgot the salvation that comes through faith and the freedom we have in Christ.

> The Greek word (metatithemi) is an interesting one. It signifies 'to transfer one's allegiance'. It is used of soldiers in the army who revolt or desert, and of men who change sides in politics or philosophy. (…) It is of this that Paul

> accuses the Galatians. They are religious turncoats, spiritual deserters. They are turning away from Him who had called them in the grace of Christ and are embracing another gospel.[3]

" I am astonished that you are so quickly deserting the one who called you to live in the grace of Christ and are turning to a different gospel—which is really no gospel at all" (Gal 1:6,7).

They were thrown into confusion (1:7)

"Evidently some people are throwing you into confusion…" (Gal 1:7)

"You foolish Galatians! Who has bewitched you? Before your very eyes Jesus Christ was clearly portrayed as crucified" (Gal 3:1).

The young Christians of these Galatian Churches have become lost and confused. So it is important for Paul to reinforce the correct teachings.

False teachers had perverted the Gospel (1:7)

"Evidently some people are throwing you into confusion and are trying to pervert the gospel of Christ" (Gal 1:7)

Paul begins by responding to the personal attacks made by the false Jewish teachers, who are sowing doubt about his ministry. Next, he reminds his readers that the law was only given to bring to light the disobedience of mankind (3:19) and to lead us to Christ through faith (3:22). He says to the readers that they are no longer "slaves" but, rather, "children" (4:7).

He urges the Galatians to abandon the Jewish law system which enslaves them, to separate themselves from these false teachers and to place their faith in Christ again, the only one who can set us free (5:1). Finally, he describes what it means to live by the Spirit.

The young Christians of Galatia had been won over by false teachers (Gal 4:17)

Paul reveals the real motivation of these false teachers: "Those people are zealous to win you over, but for no good. What they want is to alienate you from us, so that you may be zealous for them" (Gal 4:17).

These Jewish teachers have become like "gurus" for the Galatians. The Galatians were under the spell of men and not under the influence of God.

How does Paul tackle these false teachers?

- He affirms his spiritual authority in chapters 1 and 2.
- He explains the Gospel and its source again and condemns any other supposed source (chapters 3 and 4)
- He speaks of the Christian's influence and gives practical advice concerning our relationship with God, others and ourselves: the fruit of the Spirit (chapters 5 and 6)

A lesson for us today

Legalism has posed a problem for Churches down through the years and continues to do so today. It is easy to deviate from the Gospel and become caught in a straitjacket of rules and traditions. But there are other, subtler, false doctrines which can also threaten the Church. We can lose our joy and become troubled if we let ourselves be more attached to talented preachers with big personalities than to God himself.

It is therefore important that every young Christian is well acquainted with the foundations of the Christian faith: "Then we will no longer be infants, tossed back and forth by the waves, and blown here and there by every wind of teaching and by the cunning and craftiness of people in their deceitful scheming" (Eph 4:14).

So that we do not stray from the Gospel, **I would like to propose four key words** to summarise the main message of the Gospel: *justification*, *regeneration*, *sanctification* and *glorification*.

Knowing the source and the price of our salvation: justification (accepted)

"Faith is to be reckoned as righteousness to us also, who believe in him who raised from the dead our Lord Jesus Christ, who was delivered to death for our sins and raised again to secure our justification" (Ro 4.25, J.B. Phillips).

JUSTIFICATION
(ACCEPTED)

Justification : the act by which God declares that the sinner who believes becomes right in his eyes and is accepted.

God did not give up on us because of our sin. He is a just God and had to pay the full price so that we may be forgiven: "Surely he took up our pain and bore our suffering, yet we considered him punished by God, stricken by him, and afflicted. But he was pierced for our transgressions, he was crushed for our iniquities; the punishment that brought us peace was on him, and by his wounds we are healed" (Isa 53:4-5). How wonderful it is to know that we are forgiven and accepted!

Knowing the miracle of the new birth: regeneration (changed)

"Therefore, if anyone is in Christ, he is a new creation: The old has gone, the new has come!" (2Co 5:17). How wonderful it is to know the transformative power of regeneration!

REGENERATION
(CHANGED)

Regeneration : when man's nature is changed and given new life by the Holy Spirit.

Understanding the work of the Holy Spirit in our lives: sanctification (purified)

"May God himself, the God of peace, sanctify you through and through. May your whole spirit, soul and body be kept blameless at the coming of our Lord Jesus Christ. The one who calls you is faithful, and he will do it" (1Th 5:23-24).

SANCTIFICATION
(PURIFIED)

Sanctification : the constant work of the Holy Spirit within us to transform us, purify us, lead us away from evil and remake us into people who are pleasing to God.

The Word of God also plays an important role in the process of sanctification: "Christ loved the Church and gave himself up for her to make her holy, cleansing her by the washing with water through the word, and to present her to himself as a radiant Church, without stain or wrinkle or any other blemish, but holy and blameless" (Eph 5:25-26). How wonderful it is to know that the Holy Spirit is at work in my life!

Knowing the goal of our salvation: glorification

GLORIFICATION
(MADE HEIRS)

Glorification : our heavenly condition and dignity. It is our hope of eternal life.

"Moreover, we know that to those who love God, who are called according to his plan, everything that happens fits into a pattern for good. God, in his foreknowledge, chose them to bear the family likeness of his Son, that he might be the eldest of a family of many brothers. He chose them long ago; when the time came he called them, he made them righteous in his sight, and then lifted them to the splendour of life as his own sons" (Ro 8:30, J.B. Phillips).

How wonderful it is to have eternal hope!

Jesus "gave himself for our sins to rescue us from the present evil age, according to the will of our God and Father" (Gal 1:4). The Gospel proclaims deliverance and gives us access to eternal life. What great hope for the present and the future! These great truths should give us strength and put a spring in our step.

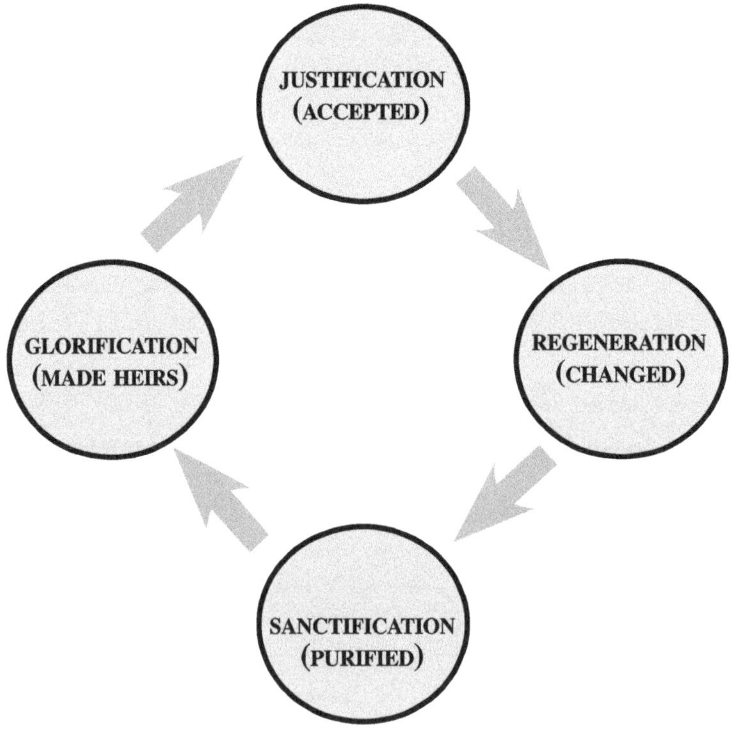

I would like to encourage you to spend some quality time studying the Word of God. At the age of 16, when I was an apprentice carpenter, I used to attend a youth Bible study group every Friday evening at my local Church. At the same time, I was also following a postal "Emmaüs" course at home. When I was 21, I went to France for one week. Chris Small, a dear English Christian friend who was working in France, said to me: "My dear Ian, I want to encourage you to spend at least one year of your life studying the Bible". I listened to him and, in the end, I dedicated eight years to my studies: four years in the ranks of Operation Mobilisation, three years at the Institut Biblique Emmaüs and one year in my Church in Larkhall in Scotland. This theoretical and practical training has been a vital and priceless investment. Even today, I need to keep learning and increasing my knowledge of the Word of God.

Take time to attend your Church's weekly bible study. Make it a priority. Consider asking your pastor or one of the elders for a personalised study session… Get a hold of some good books (there is a non-exhaustive list at the back of this book). Theology faculties and Bible colleges often offer online courses or summer classes. Have a look at what they have to offer. And why not put aside a year to study the Word of God at a Bible college?!...

The Holy Spirit: what he wants to do in our lives

To cultivate the fruit of the Spirit, you have to know the Holy Spirit and how he works.

It is thanks to the intervention of the Holy Spirit that we become Christians: "Very truly I tell you, no one can enter the kingdom of God unless they are born of water and the Spirit" (Jn 3:5). "And you also were included in Christ when you heard the message of truth, the gospel of your salvation. When you believed, you were marked in him with a seal, the promised Holy Spirit" (Eph 1:13). On the other hand, "if anyone does not have the Spirit of Christ, he does not belong to Christ" (Ro 8:9).

Jesus promises to send his Spirit: "I will ask the Father, and he will give you another advocate to help you and be with you forever—the Spirit of truth. He lives with you and will be in you" (Jn 14:16-17). This Spirit of God assures us that we are children of God (Ro 8:16) and gives us the hope of a future inheritance (Ro 8:15-17).

Remember that the Holy Spirit is a person

He gives us new life (Ro 8:13), he speaks (Ac 13:2), he consoles (Jn 14:16), he teaches us and reminds us of Christ's teachings (Jn 14:26), he convinces us of our sins (Jn 16:8), he calls on and sends missionaries (Ac 13:4), he opens and closes doors (Ac 16:6), he leads the way (Lk 4:1), he warns us (Ac 20:23), he inspires (Ac 11:28; 21:4), he sanctifies (1Co 6:11), he distributes gifts (1Co 12:9), he helps us to pray with understanding (1Co 14:15).

The Holy Spirit joins us and helps us during prayer, he helps us to pray according to God's will, he comforts us during prayer as he discerns our true needs and conveys these to God (Ro 8:26-28). He transforms us into Christ's image (2Co 3:18). He gives the ability to witness (Ac 1:8). The Holy Spirit helps us to fight and overcome sin (Ro 8:2).

We can lie to him (Ac 5:3), upset him (Eph 4:30) and resist him (Ac 6:10).

Let's open ourselves up fully to his influence and allow him to direct every aspect of our lives; let him fashion us in Christ's image by cultivating the fruit of Spirit.

MY PRAYER

Thank you, my Father, for your Holy Spirit and his work in my life. Make me sensitive to his presence in me. May he influence my thoughts, my decisions, my words and my actions. In the name of Jesus Christ, Amen.

YOUR PRAYER

— Three groups of fruit —

After reminding the Galatians that the Gospel liberates us, "In [this] freedom Christ has made us free [and completely liberated us]; stand fast then, and do not be hampered and held ensnared and submit again to a yoke of slavery [which you have once put off]" (Gal 5:1, AMPC). Paul ends his letter by speaking of the influence of a Christian led by the spirit. We are going to classify the fruits in three groups according to three different relationships.

1. Our relationship with God

God fills our hearts with love, joy and peace. This relationship will determine the strength of our other two relationships. By spending quality time in God's presence, listening to his Spirit, meditating on his Word and praying these three fruits will be developed in us. If we do not understand and cultivate this first relationship, we will have problems later on.

> *By spending quality time in God's presence, listening to his Spirit, meditating on his Word and praying, these three fruits will be developed in us.*

2. Our relationship with others

This second dimension is very important: patience, goodness and kindness. It will allow us to establish and develop strong relationships with those around us. It will help us to love people who may not seem loveable, who are difficult and who drive us up the wall! These are revolutionary fruits which allow us to achieve the impossible. These internal attitudes encourage us to listen and develop a serving spirit which will translate into actions.

3. Our relationship with ourselves

The qualities of faithfulness, gentleness and self-control will allow us to gain stability in our walk with God and to be good witnesses to those around us.

Space for reflection: questions and practical application

1. In your opinion, why is the theme of the fruit of the Spirit important?

2. Do you know the fruit of the Spirit off by heart? If not, read Galatians 5:22.

3. Evaluate your strengths and weaknesses in relation to the fruit of the Spirit.
   Give yourself a mark out of 5 for every fruit. For example, if you are very patient, put a cross in column 5 opposite patience. But if you lack gentleness, put a cross in column 1 beside gentleness and so on. Once you have completed the table, why not show it to a close friend or family member. Their opinion will be valuable and may help you to adjust your own choices if necessary.

Fruit of the Spirit	1.	2.	3.	4.	5.
Love					
Joy					
Peace					
Patience					X
Goodness					
Kindness					
Faithfulness					
Gentleness	X				
Self-control					

4. In this next table, make a note of which fruits you need to work on. For example, I lack patience, so patience will be at the top of the list and so on.

Fruit of the Spirit
Love
Joy
Peace
Patience
Goodness
Kindness
Faithfulness
Gentleness
Self-control

Fruit to work on	
1	
2	
3	
4	
5	
6	
7	
8	
9	

5. Do you know a Christian who demonstrates the fruit of the Spirit? What impact have they had on you and others around them?

— Love —

"But the fruit of the Spirit is **love**, joy, peace, patience, kindness, goodness, faithfulness, gentleness and self-control" (Galatians 5:22)

Definition in the *Oxford English Dictionary*: "A feeling or disposition of deep affection or fondness for someone, typically arising from a recognition of attractive qualities, from natural affinity, or from sympathy and manifesting itself in concern for the other's welfare and pleasure in his or her presence".

> "The word love is often abused these days. It is used in the context of close, cosy feelings; of ecstatic, exuberant sexual passion; and of conditional commitments ("I'll love you if you live up to my expectations").[4]

Films, the theatre, books and the internet bombard us with images of this kind of love. And we enjoy it, don't we?

> *"Love is not an affectionate feeling, but a steady wish for the loved person's ultimate good as far as it can be obtained."*
> C.S. Lewis

Here, we are going to examine a completely different kind of love.

C.S. Lewis gave a lovely definition: "Love is not an affectionate feeling, but a steady wish for the loved person's ultimate good as far as it can be obtained."[5]

> "One day, Saint Augustine was asked: "What does love look like?" He replied: "It has hands to help others. It has feet to

> hasten towards the poor and needy. It has eyes to see misery and hardship. It has ears to hear people's sighs and woes. This is what love looks like".[6]

In classical Greek, the word "love" has four possible meanings:

"*Eros*" A passionate physical love between two people.

"*Philia*" A feeling of affection which links intimate friends.

"*Storge*" Affection which links family members: parents and children.

"'*Agape'*, the Christian word, means unconquerable benevolence. It means that, no matter what people may do to us by way of insult or injury or humiliation, we will never seek anything else but their highest good. It is therefore a feeling of the mind as much as of the heart; it concerns the will as much as the emotions."[7]

The quality of "agape", which is referred to a lot in the New Testament, characterises the love which God has for man (Jn 3:16, 1Jn 4:8-9) and love between humans (Mt 22:39).

The Bible gives us a wonderful definition of true love in 1 Corinthians 13:1-13:

> If I speak with the eloquence of men and of angels, but have no love, I become no more than blaring brass or crashing cymbal. If I have the gift of foretelling the future and hold in my mind not only all human knowledge but the very secrets of God, and if I also have that absolute faith which can move mountains, but have no love, I amount to nothing at all. If I dispose of all that I possess, yes, even if I give my own body to be burned, but have no love, I achieve precisely nothing. This love of which I speak is slow to lose patience—it looks for a way of being constructive. It is not possessive: it is neither anxious to impress nor does it cherish inflated ideas of its own importance.
>
> Love has good manners and does not pursue selfish advantage. It is not touchy. It does not keep account of evil or

gloat over the wickedness of other people. On the contrary, it is glad with all good men when truth prevails.
Love knows no limit to its endurance, no end to its trust, no fading of its hope; it can outlast anything. It is, in fact, the one thing that still stands when all else has fallen.
All gifts except love will be superseded one day.
For if there are prophecies they will be fulfilled and done with, if there are "tongues" the need for them will disappcar, if there is knowledge it will be swallowed up in truth. For our knowledge is always incomplete and our prophecy is always incomplete, and when the complete comes, that is the end of the incomplete.
When I was a little child I talked and felt and thought like a little child. Now that I am a man my childish speech and feeling and thought have no further significance for me.
At present we are men looking at puzzling reflections in a mirror. The time will come when we shall see reality whole and face to face! At present all I know is a little fraction of the truth, but the time will come when I shall know it as fully as God now knows me!
In this life we have three great lasting qualities—faith, hope and love. But the greatest of them is love" (J.B. Phillips).

This beautiful passage on "agape" love mentions other fruits of the Spirit like patience and kindness... but also some of the gifts of the Spirit (v.8) such as prophecies, tongues and knowledge... To exercise these gifts, love is essential.

Juan Carlos Ortiz said: "Love is the oxygen of the kingdom."[8]

This "agape" love is not humanly possible. We already know that our love, depending on the situations or the people we face, is like elastic. Have you ever stretched an elastic band? It can stretch pretty far but, eventually, it will snap and break. Our love for others may be great but it will reach its limit at one time or another.

Here is a small test to evaluate the love you have for your neighbour: imagine that your next-door neighbour knocks on your door and asks you for a packet of flour to make a cake. You are happy to oblige. Bravo!

The next week, the same person knocks on your door: "I have a serious problem; my bank account has gone into deficit. Would you be able to lend me £1,500?" Being generous, you withdraw that amount from your account and give it to him. Well done again!

Sometime later, your neighbour is in a car crash. The hospital contacts you because the patient needs an organ donation and it seems that you are compatible: you can give him the organ he needs. Would you be willing to give him a part of your body?

To love beyond our limits we need a power which is not our own, don't we? – the love of God in our hearts.

Love: at the heart of God and the Gospel

"God is love" (1Jn 4:8, 16). This affirmation, which is repeated several times in the Bible, is one of the Bible's most extraordinary declarations. It is love which "determines the internal relationship between the Father, the Son and the Holy Spirit as well as the external relationship between the Creator and his creatures (Jn 17:23)".[9]

The love of God is at the heart of the Gospel: "For **God so loved the world** that he gave his one and only Son..." (Jn 3:16). This love extends to every nation, to everyone throughout the world.

> It is staggering that God should love sinners; yet it is true. God loves creatures who have become unlovely and [...] unlovable. [...] Love among persons is awakened by something in the beloved, but the love of God is free, spontaneous, unevoked, uncaused.[10]

God's love is already in our hearts

We cannot produce this love. The Christian receives it in his heart when he is converted.

"Therefore, since we have been justified through faith, we have peace with God through our Lord Jesus Christ [...] God's love has been poured out into our hearts through the Holy Spirit, who has been given to us.[...] God demonstrates his own love for us in this: While we were still sinners, Christ died for us" (Ro 5:1-8).

When Paul says that "God's love has been poured out into our hearts", "it suggests a free flow and a large quantity – in fact, an inundation [...] Paul is not talking of faint and fitful impressions, but of deep and overwhelming ones."[11]

Love is the foundation for cultivating the other fruits of the Spirit

Love is at the beginning of the list of fruits: it is the most important. Without love, the other fruits cannot exist.

For a short period in my life, I worked as a carpenter/joiner. I would arrive with my colleagues at the building site in a truck loaded with beams and joists to erect the roof. I have never put a roof on unless the foundations and walls were already in place. Love is the foundation upon which other fruits can be expressed. Be careful not to put the "cart before the horse" or the roof before the foundations and walls!

> *When Paul says that "God's love has been poured out into our hearts", "it suggests a free flow and a large quantity – in fact, an inundation".* J. Packer

Loving is a commandment

Surprising, isn't it! It is as much an act of the will as an emotion, as mentioned earlier.

"'Love the Lord your God with all your heart and with all your soul and with all your mind.' This is the first and greatest commandment. And the second is like it: 'Love your neighbour as yourself'" (Mt 22:37-39). Here, Jesus quotes the Old Testament.

Within this commandment, there are three dimensions - the three relationships which we came across in Galatians in relation to the fruits:

- Our relationship with God: "Love the Lord your God".
- Our relationship with others: "Love your neighbour".
- Our relationship with ourselves: "as yourself" or "as you love yourself".

"Dear friends, since God so loved us, we also ought to love one another" (1Jn 4:11). You will notice that

> the love of God and the love of our neighbour are inseparable. We see the result, primarily, from the way in which Jesus links the one to the other. He was asked which commandment was the most important. He could say: "Love the Lord your God" and stop there, since that is the most important commandment. But he did not want to mention the first commandment without immediately adding the second [...]: "Love your neighbour" (Matt 22:37-39). The apostle John takes a similar approach: "And he has given us this command: Anyone who loves God must also love their brother and sister" (1 John 4:21).[12]

Jesus reminds us that love is the distinctive mark of the Christian: "By this everyone will know that you are my disciples, if you love one another" (Jn 13:35).

To love: four subjects for prayer

Paul prays for the Church at Ephesus (Eph 3:16-19) and gives us four subjects for prayer in relation to God's love: power – motivation – understanding – experience:

> "I pray that out of his glorious riches he [God] may strengthen you with power through his Spirit in your inner being, so that Christ may dwell in your hearts through faith. And I pray that you, being rooted and established in love, may have power, together with all the Lord's holy people,

> to grasp how wide and long and high and deep is the love of Christ, and to know this love that surpasses knowledge—that you may be filled to the measure of all the fullness of God."

Power: "I pray that [...] [God] may strengthen you" (v.16). We require a divine power to love beyond our own limitations. This power is communicated to us by the working of the Holy Spirit in our hearts.

Motivation: "being rooted and established in love" (v.17). These two words, rooted and established, evoke the idea of nourishment and stability. To build up, you first have to dig deep. Christians must be strongly rooted in Christ's love: this is our motivation to love others. "If God loved us as much as that, surely we, in our turn, should love each other!" (1Jn 4:11).

Understanding: "I pray that you [...] grasp how wide and long and high and deep is the love of Christ, and know this love that surpasses knowledge" (v.17-19). Paul gives us its dimensions:

- Length: it is eternal
- Depth: it wrests the worst sinners from the depths of hell
- Height: it reaches as far as the heavens into Christ's presence
- Width: it embraces all of humanity throughout the centuries

We know that a table has three dimensions, for example: its length, height and width. If Christ's love is four dimensional, it is divine and beyond our understanding. Are we responsible for the miracle of Christ's presence in our hearts?! It is not a question of our love for God but, rather, of God's love for us. That changes everything.

Experience: "that you may be filled to the measure of all the fullness of God" (v.19). This expression suggests that the believer must realise that he needs to make use of God's infinite resources, and treasures of grace. What amazing potential exists in being filled with the Holy Spirit and cultivating the fruit of love.

When I was a carpenter, I worked with some old craftsmen in a workshop. Once a week, I would train in a specialist school. Until that point, putting on a roof involved many people hoisting each joist and placing it in its definitive place; traces were made on the wood with the exact angle for cutting; it was then brought down to be cut. What a task! It was a difficult and delicate operation.

One day at the specialist school of building, our teacher gave us a mathematical formula. Working from a plan, he asked us to cut the joist to the correct length and angle without getting on a roof. He gave the students a demonstration and it was perfect! What a discovery! What a surprise it was for the old craftsmen the next day on the building site when, using the mathematical formula, I was able to demonstrate how to cut the joist without getting on the roof!

Knowing mathematical formulas is very useful but being able to apply them in everyday life is even better.

Paul's formula to allow God's love to overflow in our own hearts is in Ephesians 3:16:

power + motivation + understanding + experience.

Let's take it and apply it!

God's love in our hearts expresses itself in the family

The Bible emphasises the importance of love within the family:

- The love of a husband for his wife (Eph 5:28).
- The love of a wife for her husband and children (Tit 2:4).
- The love of children for their parents (Eph 6:2).

If it is true that our love for Jesus must be the priority (Lk 13:34), anyone who does not take care of their own relatives is considered an "worse than an unbeliever" (1Ti 5:8). God created the family before he created the Church.

God's love in our hearts expresses itself in the local Church

> "Jesus told his disciples to love one another (John 13:34), and in the New Testament emphasis is placed on brotherly love. We do not always agree on every point with other Christians, but that does not prevent us from having a special connection with them as they have been saved by the same Saviour and are led by the same Spirit."[13]

The apostle Paul prays that the Christians of Ephesus may understand the love of Christ (Eph 3:18-19). He prays for the Philippian Church that their "love may abound more and more" (Php 1:9). He also gives a lot of attention to love in the introductions to his letters. For the Thessalonian Church, Paul expresses this wish: "May the Lord direct your hearts into God's love" (2Th 3:5); to the Church in Rome he says: "neither height nor depth, nor anything else in all creation, will be able to separate us from the love of God" (Ro 8:39).

There are no solitary Christians in the Bible. I would like to encourage each of you to find a spiritual family, a Church which teaches you how to receive and share the love of God. There have been times when I have prayed for Christians whom I struggled to love. I prayed for them and never saw them in the same way again. They had not changed but my way of looking at them had been modified, for prayer allows us to see the other through God's eyes. When we pray for our brothers and sisters, it creates a bond of affection between our hearts. This is the miracle of prayer: love drives out selfishness and the spirit of comparison and competition to unite our hearts.

> *Prayer enables us to see others through God's eyes, and creates a bond of affection between our hearts.*

God's love in our hearts expresses itself in every situation

It was the source and driving power of the apostle Paul's motivation: "For Christ's love *compels* us, because we are convinced that one died for all, and therefore all died" (2Co 5:14). The Amplified version translates this verse as "the love of God controls *and* urges *and* impels us".

Our love must extend well beyond our small family or Church circle. It must touch our friends, our colleagues at work...

During a stay on the Logos Hope, Operation Mobilisation's ship, in Asia, we saw a group of young people with huge rucksacks on their backs leave early one morning. I asked them: "where are you going like that?" "We are going into the jungle for ten days to spread the Gospel to tribes who have never heard of Jesus." What enthusiasm! And the secret to their motivation? Christ's love which drove them forward!

A revolutionary love

Loving lovable people is easy. But our love must extend far beyond this to those who are difficult, who do not love us, who do not seek to cultivate the fruit of the Spirit...

Once I liberate God's love, I can rejoice in this love and let it flow freely.

Personally, I am more at ease with the Old Testament phrase: "an eye for an eye, a tooth for a tooth". It is logical. If someone slaps my left cheek, I slap their right cheek and we are even. But when we turn to the New Testament, this has changed completely. Jesus says, "love your enemies, and pray for those who hate you". He sets the bar very high! But this is possible thanks to the presence and power of the Holy Spirit in our hearts. Once I liberate God's love, I can rejoice in this love and let it flow freely.

A love which gives

Love is not restricted to beautiful words. It must be put into practice: "let us not love with words or speech but with actions and in truth" (1Jn 3:18). We can actively bear witness to our brothers and sisters through our attentiveness and, as a result, prove the sincerity of our love for God.

God's love is not just an emotion, it is also a love which expresses itself, which gives: "For God so loved the world that **he gave** his one and only Son" (Jn 3:16).

God's love is a love which embodies itself in reality. It is a love which comes down to us, to meet us in our difficulties. It is a love which speaks, which takes action, which touches and transforms.

> *"You can give without loving, but you cannot love without giving."*
> Amy Carmichael

Throughout the Bible, we witness the generosity of this God of love. From creation, he gives a garden to cultivate, leaders to guide and liberate; he gives prophets to instruct, correct and encourage. He gives his Son to save us. He gives us his Spirit to guide and console us. He gives us his Word to strengthen and enlighten us. He gives his Church to protect us and help us grow in our faith…

God's love gives. Filled with this love, we can also give to others: it could be a word of kindness to a sick friend, a favour for a neighbour, time spent with our children or grandchildren…

I like this quotation from Amy Carmichael: "You can give without loving, but you cannot love without giving."[14]

A Scottish home which radiated God's love – a reality!

I would like, briefly, to bear witness to my Christian parents. My father was a fishmonger. He ran, along with my mother, nine fish shops in the Glasgow, Lanarkshire area. This business required a lot of time and energy… But my father, in spite of his hectic schedule (he started at 5am and did not finish till late in the evening), never missed a Church service or meeting: Bible studies, prayer meetings or Sunday services. And he still found time to look after the flowers outside the Church.

He took time every morning to get on his knees and pray for our family. So many gestures expressing God's love.

My mother had the gift of hospitality. We often had guests staying with us (preachers, members of the Salvation Army's brass band, gypsies…) and we almost always had guests at the dinner table on Sundays. My mother was very busy during the week with the shop staff, but she always found time for us, her children. There were three of us. Before leaving for school each morning, she would read us a Bible verse and take us on her knee to pray.

She was interested in people who were rejected by society, like gypsies, or people who were vulnerable through disability. I still remember the apartment we had in a working-class area in Larkhall, south of Glasgow. We often heard screaming and crying coming from the neighbouring apartment. My mother quickly realised what was happening: a young girl who was deaf and dumb was being mistreated by her parents. Theresa was often deprived of food and hit for the smallest thing. My mother alerted social services to the problem. When the investigation was taking place and Theresa's parents were absent, she brought Theresa home to look after her, feed her and show her affection. She even went to sign language classes so that she could communicate with Theresa. The young girl was finally placed in a special residential school. For many years, my mother continued to visit her and encourage her in her plans for the future.

This selfless love, which wanted nothing in return, struck me in the same way as the importance of prayer in my parents' lives did. It bore fruit as it sowed a passion for prayer in my own heart.

The young boy crying in a train station – a true story

I am very fond of this story and it will help us to understand the love of God. It is a true story which takes place in Euston Station in London (a station I know well as the link between Glasgow and London).

In this large station in the north of London, there is a young boy who needs to take a train. He is perhaps 12-13 years old; he is alone and he seems to have a problem: he is crying. A rich gentleman arrives at the same station and, seeing the boy crying, he approaches him and takes an interest in him. This makes us think of Jesus who left heaven to meet us, speak with us, understand us, help us, console us and, most importantly, save us.

The gentleman leans towards the young boy and says: "what's the matter, son?" The boy, still crying, responds: "I've lost my ticket". "Look here, said the man, I will buy you a ticket on one condition: if you ever find yourself in a station and see a young child crying because he has lost his ticket, you will look after him. How does that sound?". "Yes sir!" replies the child.

This man's love is a *practical love* because he puts his hand in his pocket, takes out his wallet and pays for a ticket. It is an *authentic love* because there was nothing forcing him to help the boy. Jesus paid with his own body, he gave his life for us. He came voluntarily into the world to save us as sinners. And finally, it is a *revolutionary love* because, for the rest of his life, this boy will try to help unfortunate children lost in train stations. Christians, touched by the love of Christ, are invited to spread the good news of the Gospel to the ends of the earth.

As the train moves away from the platform, the young boy lowers his window, attracts the gentleman's attention and shouts to him "Hey Sir, I will do for others what you have done for me!" Jesus says to us: "I gave my life for you. It's up to you to spread this love to others".

In the words of the apostle Paul, this is my prayer for you, dear reader:

> "My prayer for you is that you may have still more love—a love that is full of knowledge and wise insight. I want you to be able always to recognise the highest and the best, and to live sincere and blameless lives until the day of Jesus Christ. I want to see your lives full of true goodness, produced by the power that Jesus Christ gives you to the praise and glory of God". (Php 1:9, J.B. Phillips)

Space for reflection: questions and practical application

1. Why is the search for love so important in songs, books and films?

2. What is the source of true love (Jn 4:7-11)?

3. I thought love was an emotion but, in John 13:34-35, Jesus tells us it is a commandment to love one another. Explain?

4. Where should my motivation to accept and love unlovable people come from (1Jn 4:7-19)?

5. Jesus goes even further: he asks us to pray for our enemies (Mt 5:44). What takes place in our hearts when we pray for them?

6. How can I express my love in practical ways for someone close to me: family, neighbours, work colleagues? What can I do? For whom? When can I do it?

Meditation and prayer

Take time to meditate on the immensity of God's love as it is expressed in this hymn. Contemplate the dimensions of God's love: its length, width, depth and height (Eph 3:14-20).

The love of God is greater far
Than tongue or pen can ever tell.
It goes beyond the highest star
And reaches to the lowest hell.
The guilty pair, bowed down with care,
God gave His Son to win;
His erring child He reconciled
And pardoned from his sin

O love of God, how rich and pure!
How measureless and strong!
It shall forevermore endure
The saints' and angels' song.

Could we with ink the ocean fill,
And were the skies of parchment made;
Were every stalk on earth a quill,
And every man a scribe by trade;
To write the love of God above
Would drain the ocean dry;
Nor could the scroll contain the whole,
Though stretched from sky to sky.[15]

MY PRAYER

Lord, I am loved and forgiven by the greatest love possible. I pray that I will be touched by your Holy Spirit and that I will radiate your love to those around me today. Amen.

YOUR PRAYER

— Joy —

"But the fruit of the Spirit is love, **joy**, peace, patience, kindness, goodness, faithfulness, gentleness and self-control" (Galatians 5:22)

The dictionary tells us that joy is: "A vivid emotion of pleasure arising from a sense of well-being or satisfaction; the feeling or state of being highly pleased or delighted; exultation of spirit; gladness, delight."

The biblical dictionary tells us that "Joy is an enjoyable and profound emotion. It can be linked to a particular cause [...]. Joy is also the state of someone who has a clear conscience"[16] and therefore, also, a sense of inner peace.

We have all experienced this kind of joy: going home with good grades, passing an exam, getting our first salary, asking for our loved one's hand in marriage, learning that our wife is pregnant, that we have received a promotion, etc.

To my knowledge, joy is the only thing which, when shared with others, doubles, triples or, indeed, quadruples in value. You have surely had the uplifting experience of sharing good news over the phone!

Seeking joy: misguided approaches

"Even in laughter the heart may ache, and rejoicing may end in grief" (Pr 14:13).

I have just finished reading a book by Frédéric Lenoir, *La puissance de la joie* (*The Power of Joy*).[17] In this work, the

> *To my knowledge, joy is the only thing which, when shared with others, doubles, triples or, indeed, quadruples in value.*

author analyses different philosophical interpretations of joy: Spinoza, Nietzsche, Bergson... and suggests different ways by which we can obtain joy: Buddhist meditation, letting go, self-awareness, searching, freeing the joy that is within us, etc. The problem with this kind of joy is that it depends on us. We have to create it, seek it, maintain it and does not last.

"When you jump for joy, beware that no one moves the ground from beneath your feet."[18] This humourous quotation from Stanislaw J. Lec is very good advice in relation to the misguided suggestions above. This kind of joy is fleeting and based on circumstances. It will disappear at the slightest hint of irritation or conflict.

Worshipping celebrities: Procuring a kind of joy from worshipping a successful person or star. We are also in danger of doing this in the Christian world. So many people chase after the most popular speaker...

Worshipping material goods: I recently heard someone say: "I was feeling down in the dumps so I bought myself a pair of shoes". We all know that material goods can only give us momentary joy and that this kind of pursuit of happiness is endless.

Worshipping our own acts of service to God: I get immense pleasure from what I do; studying the Word of God and sharing it with others. But be careful! There is a risk that I could become proud, cling to my successes and make them the source of my joy.

During my pastoral ministry, I had a bookstall in the market for almost thirty years in a place called Pierrelatte, in the south of France. I sold only Bibles. I knew all the stallholders around me: on my left, Mireille sold socks, on my right, Jacques sold fabric. I sold, on average, one Bible a week. I sometimes became disheartened because my joy was dependent on my sales.

One morning, I was behind my bookstall and started counting the number of people passing each minute: around forty-nine people. They stopped to buy socks and cloth, but no one stopped at my bookstall. I was discouraged.

Sometime before, Mireille had asked me if I could look after her stall whilst she went for a coffee. I was happy to do so and sold several pairs of socks that morning. The next week, Jacques who sold cloth, asked me the same favour. I managed to sell quite a lot of cloth.

One morning when I was disheartened, I had the inspired idea to ask Mireille and Jacques to look after my stall to allow me to have a short coffee break. A little hesitant at first as they said they did not know much about the Bible, they eventually agreed.

I could see them from a distance from the cafe terrace: Mireille and Jacques behind my book table, opening the Bible, explaining it to people who stopped to ask questions. When I returned to the book table, I was so surprised to hear that Mireille and Jacques (non- Christians) had sold three Bibles!

In all my 30 years of experience at the market, I had never sold three Bibles in one morning!

I tell this story to show how God watches over us, that he is always there, particularly when we are feeling disheartened. God showed me that I needed to persevere, that I should not put my hope in others or results, but that my joy is in him and his ability to do "immeasurably more than all we ask or imagine" (Eph 3:20). God sometimes acts without us.

What does it matter how many Bibles were sold? God wants us to find our joy in Him.

I had often asked the Church to pray for me and my activity at the market. When I shared my experience with them, we prayed that God would help me to persevere, with my joy centred on him and not circumstances. When you feel discouraged, do not hesitate to tell a friend, who will pray that you might find true joy in God once more.

The meaning and place of joy in the Bible

Joy is a subject that is given great importance in the Bible and it is referenced around a hundred and twenty times.

It appears right from creation, "while the morning stars sang together and all the angels shouted for joy?" (Job 38:7). Joy existed well before the creation of man: "Where were you when I laid the earth's foundation?" asks God. Our God is a joyful God. In some Christian circles, joy has been banished because of legalism! When these people come out of the Church, it looks as though they have been baptised in lemon juice! No! God created his people to be joyful: "I will create Jerusalem to be a delight and its people a joy" (Isa 65:18).

On some occasions, God himself participates in this joy: "I will rejoice over Jerusalem and take delight in my people" (Isa 65:19).

Joy, in the Bible, is an enjoyable and profound emotion. It can be linked to a particular cause (an event, a present, a party) but, above all, it is a state of inner well-being. God is the object of this joy: his person, his attributes and his saving grace.

"You turned my wailing into dancing; you removed my sackcloth and clothed me with joy" (Ps 30:11); "For the kingdom of God is not a matter of eating and drinking, but of righteousness, peace and joy in the Holy Spirit" (Ro 14:17). "May the God of hope fill you with all joy and peace as you trust in him, so that you may overflow with hope by the power of the Holy Spirit" (Ro 15:13). This profound joy comes from God and is communicated to us by the Holy Spirit.

> *"May the God of hope fill you with joy and peace in your faith, that by the power of the Holy Spirit, your whole life and outlook may be radiant with hope".*
> *(Rom 15:13, J.B. Phillips)*

The source of joy

God himself

C.H. Spurgeon said: "Joy in God is the happiest of all joys."[19]

Our inner well-being is nourished by God himself, his presence, his works and his Word. This is the crux of the matter: God is our main source of joy. Our hearts experience profound joy when we come to understand God himself, the person of God.

"I will give thanks to you, LORD, with all my heart; I will tell of all your wonderful deeds. **I will be glad and rejoice in you**; I will sing the praises of your name, O Most High" (Ps 9:1-2). When our lives are centred on God, plunged into his presence, we can access real joy.

> Charles H. Spurgeon, the prince of preachers, said: "Then go, plunge yourself in the Godhead's deepest sea; be lost in his immensity and you shall come forth as from a couch of rest, refreshed and invigorated."[20]

"You will **fill me with joy in your presence**" (Ps 16:11). "**My soul will rejoice in the Lord** and delight in his salvation" (Ps 35:9).

David invites us to rejoice:

"Come, let us sing for joy to the LORD;
let us shout aloud to the Rock of our salvation.
Let us come before him with thanksgiving
and extol him with music and song.

For the LORD is the great God,
the great King above all gods.
In his hand are the depths of the earth,
and the mountain peaks belong to him.
The sea is his, for he made it,
and his hands formed the dry land.

Come, let us bow down in worship,
let us kneel before the Lord *our Maker;*
for he is our God
and we are the people of his pasture,
the flock under his care" (Ps 95:1-7).

What a wonderful passage! Note the source of his joy: his great God. Martin Luther said to his friend Spalatin one day: "You have a problem. Your God is too small." What size is your God? Is he as large as your bathroom? Your garden? Or is he the God of the universe?

I am not very fond of the word "praise". I prefer the word "worship". Sometimes when we say in our Churches "now we are going to take a moment for praise", people begin to pray about anything and everything: for a grandmother who is having trouble with her knees, for a missionary working in Africa and then it moves on to repentance. But that is not what worship means. It is a prayer centred on the person of God. David expresses it well in Psalm 22:26: "those who seek the Lord will praise him". Praise and worship are the locomotive of prayer. Behind come the other carriages: confession, intercession, thanksgiving, etc.

Constantly working to know God better is essential. It is this knowledge of God which creates joy in our hearts. Albert Einstein said: "Knowing God, this is the key for Christians, the rest is just details".

Once a week, early in the morning I get in my car to go and pray in a forest. With me, I take a list of God's attributes which I have found in the Bible (I currently have a hundred and sixty-four).

In my book, *Back to Basics, back to God*[21], I suggest several practical exercises to make the attributes of God the foundation of our prayers. I will base my prayer on one of these attributes and, after this time spent in intimacy with God, I will emerge with my heart filled with a profound joy.

Centred on Jesus and his works

We have seen in the Old Testament that God is the source of joy and I would like to emphasise that our joy is also to be found in Jesus.

> *"I have told you this so that my joy may be in you and that your joy may be complete" (John 15:11).*

This joy is announced by the prophets and the angels at the time of Jesus' birth: "I bring you good news that will cause great joy for all the people" (Lk 2:10). It is in Jesus himself and his work that we find this perfect, profound and complete joy (Jn 15:11), even in our trials (Jas 1:2).

When Jesus carried out miracles: "the whole crowd of disciples began joyfully to praise God in loud voices for all the miracles they had seen" (Lk 19:37).

In John 15, when Jesus urges us to remain in him, he declares: "I have told you this so that my joy may be in you and that your joy may be complete" (Jn 15:11).

The salvation we have in Jesus

"Rejoice that your names are written in heaven" (Lk 10:20).

Meditation on God's Word

"When your words came, I ate them; **they were my joy and my heart's delight**, for I bear your name, LORD God Almighty" (Jer 15:16).

Psalm 119, which is a hymn celebrating God's Word, begins with this expression "Happy":

"Happy are those whose lives are faultless,
who live according to the law of the LORD.
Happy are those who follow his commands" (GNT)

Later, in verse 111, the Psalmist says:

"Your commandments are my eternal possession;
they are the joy of my heart". (GNT)

How wonderful it is to open the Bible, read it, meditate on it and let God speak to us!

> *I will base my prayer on one of these attributes and, after this time spent in intimacy with God, I will emerge with my heart filled with a profound joy.*

My life is punctuated with small and large joys, like playing Bach's Prelude on the piano by heart and without any mistakes; making an oak door from scratch: putting it through the circular saw, making the mortices and tenons, gluing it all together with clamps, sanding it down, varnishing it and putting it on its hinges; walking in the mountains of Glencoe in Scotland… But I think that my greatest joy is when a word or verse from the Bible really strikes a chord and lights a flame in my heart. The disciples, on their way to Emmaus, knew this when Jesus, risen from the dead, explained to them what was said in all the scriptures concerning himself. They said to one another: "Were not our hearts burning within us while he talked with us on the road and opened the Scriptures to us?" (Lk 24:32).

God's intervention for us

"My soul glorifies the Lord and my spirit rejoices in God my Saviour […] for the Mighty One has done great things for me" (Lk 1:46-49).

My wife Françoise and I chose this verse for our son's birth announcement. We were filled with joy and grateful that God had blessed us, after five years of marriage, with this much longed-for child who, for a long time, we had eagerly awaited.

Some years later, we were able to adopt a little four-year-old girl from Thailand. What joy!

I would like to encourage you to take a blank sheet of paper, to write down everything that Jesus has done for you and thank him for it.

The characteristics of this joy

A joy that lasts

"I will make you the everlasting pride and the joy of all generations" (Isa 60:15).

"But let all who take refuge in you be glad; let them ever sing for joy. Spread your protection over them, that those who love your name may rejoice in you" (Ps 5:11).

"Those the Lord has rescued will return. They will enter Zion with singing; everlasting joy will crown their heads. Gladness and joy will overtake them, and sorrow and sighing will flee away" (Isa 35:10).

This joy, this fruit of the Spirit, is eternal.

A joy which expresses itself

In the Old Testament, national holidays, sacrificial ceremonies or military victories were popular occasions of jubilation, along with family celebrations: marriages, circumcisions... This joy was expressed through shouts of joy, songs, music, dancing...

"Let Israel rejoice in their Maker; let the people of Zion be glad in their King. Let them praise his name with dancing and make music to him with tambourine and harp" (Ps 149:2-3).

The people of Israel were sensitive to the presence of God, to his protection and provision and they praised him for that (Ps 96:1-12).

Sing to the Lord a new song;
sing to the Lord, all the earth.
Sing to the Lord, praise his name;
proclaim his salvation day after day.

Declare his glory among the nations,
his marvellous deeds among all people. [...]

Let the heavens rejoice, let the earth be glad;
let the sea resound, and all that is in it.
Let the fields be jubilant, and everything in them;
let all the trees of the forest sing for joy.

What a symphony!

The call to come together to rejoice in the presence of the Eternal is magnificent here: peoples, nations, inhabitants of the earth. Even creation is invited to join the celebrations (heavens, earth, sea – v.11-12).

"Bring an offering and come into his courts" (v.8). The offering was, and still is, a time of joy when everyone, in a spirit of gratitude, gave back a portion of their goods to the Lord. We know that "It is more blessed to give than to receive" (Ac 20:35). We recently gave a friend of ours a computer as a gift. What joy! Each time that we have made a donation to a Christian charity or to a servant of the Lord, it has brought us such joy!

In the Hebrew calendar, Israel celebrated seven religious festivals, all established by God himself. The religious year began in spring. During these festivals, which sometimes lasted a week, the people abandoned themselves to worshipping and joy. These celebrations still take place nowadays Leviticus 23:1-44 gives us information about these festivals, the reason for them and their duration.

Passover: festival to commemorate the deliverance from Egypt; particularly the passing of God's angel over the houses, saving those whose door lintels were covered with the blood of a lamb.

Feast of unleavened bread: festival connected with the preceding festival and which lasted a week.

Feast of Weeks: a festival which was celebrated seven weeks after Passover (Pentecost for the first Church).

Feast of First fruits: festival to thank God after the harvest, with offerings of sheaves of wheat and sacrifices. This makes us think of the "Harvest festival" in English speaking countries when believers bring fruits and vegetables to thank God for his provision.

Feast of Trumpets (New Year): festival to symbolise the future coming together of the people of Israel. A day of rest and sacrifices.

Day of Atonement: day of humiliation and repentance accompanied by fasting.

Festival of Tabernacles: seven days of rest in tents (or huts) with sacrifices.

The Jewish festivals were a prefiguration of the salvation to come, "a shadow of the things that were to come", according to Colossians 2:17. For us, who have been brought to fullness in Christ (v.10.), each day is a day of celebration!

The benefits of joy

> *"the joy of the Lord is your strength" (Ne 8:10)*

Inner strength

Nehemiah tells us that "the joy of the Lord is your strength" (Neh 8:10). Yet, Nehemiah did not have an easy life: he was attacked from all sides: from without and within. But he held on! How? Because the joy of God was his strength. His secret? He knew his God and, in prayer, trusted in him completely (Ne 1:5-11).

Thanks to this joy, his strength, he was able to undertake a colossal task: reconstructing the walls of Jerusalem in fifty-one days.

Help during times of trial

> "Consider it pure joy, my brothers and sisters, whenever you face trials of many kinds, because you know that the testing

of your faith produces perseverance. Let perseverance finish its work so that you may be mature and complete, not lacking anything" (Jas 1:2-4).

How is it possible to be so joyful in difficult times?

Paul says something similar in Romans 5:3: "we also glory in our sufferings". Why? Because these trials produce patience, perseverance and spiritual maturity.

We also see, in the book of Acts, that the apostles preached the Word with joy and full assurance even though they were threatened with persecution (Ac 4:29). What an example for us! When we share the Word of God, even in hostile territory, we can have joy in our hearts knowing that the Word of God always bears fruit: "my word that goes out from my mouth [...]will not return to me empty" (Isa 55:11).

A means to spread the Gospel

"The Christian is the man of joy (...) A gloomy Christian is a contradiction in terms, and nothing in all religious history has done Christianity more harm than its connection with black clothes and long faces."[22]

This quotation is attributed to Saint Augustine: "The Christian should be an alleluia from head to foot".[23]

Jesus prays for his disciples: "that they may have the full measure of my joy within them" (Jn 17:13). Later, he adds: "My prayer is not for them alone. I pray also for those who will believe in me through their message" (v.20). At the start of Acts, we see that the apostles are filled with this joy.

"And day after day they regularly assembled in the temple with united purpose, and in their homes they broke bread [including the Lord's Supper]. They partook of their food with gladness and simplicity *and* generous hearts" (Ac 2.46, AMPC).

My grand-mother was a joyful Christian. When I was a child, I admired her laughing eyes and her "banana" smile! She radiated the joy of the Lord when she prayed. It was she who first kindled the passion for prayer in my heart. She made you want to imitate her. She bore witness to her faith to everyone she met and knew how to pass on the joy which the good news of the Gospel produces.

Other sources of joy

The Church

"I rejoiced with those who said to me, 'Let us go to the house of the Lord" (Ps 122:1). He rejoices because God is present, not in the building, but through the Holy Spirit in the hearts of his brothers and sisters, and in a very special way when we worship God. "You are the one Israel praises" (Ps 22:3). I remember a time when, in Avignon, we invited our neighbours to come to a Church service. It was the first time they had set foot in an evangelical, protestant Church. They later shared with us that what had touched them most was not the preaching, but the time of praise, prayers and singing, when they specially felt the presence of God and the joy of the Christians.

Joy is a hallmark of the New Testament Church "They broke bread in their homes and ate together with glad and sincere hearts" (Ac 2:46). The disciples receive this joy with the Holy Spirit (Ac 13:52) and it accompanies the miracles: "there was great joy in that city" (Ac 8:7).

Paul prays that the Colossians may be strengthened and experience true joy: "May you be made strong with all the strength which comes from his glorious power, so that you may be able to endure everything with patience. And with joy give thanks to the Father, who has made you fit to have your share of what God has reserved for his people in the kingdom of light" (Col 1:11, GNT).

The progress of other Christians

Paul describes the Thessalonian Christians as: "our glory and joy" (1Th 2:20). It is the progress of these Christians which gives him great joy. The strengthened Christians of the Philippian Church are also a source of joy for Paul: "Therefore, my brothers and sisters, you whom I love and long for, my joy and crown, stand firm in the Lord in this way, dear friends!" (Php 4:1). In my Church planting ministry, my greatest joy has been to witness people becoming Christians. When I think of everyone who has been touched by the Gospel and has asked to be baptised, whom I have seen grow in their faith and take on responsibilities in the Church... it fills me with joy, even today. Like the apostle John, I can say: "I have no greater joy than to hear that my children are walking in the truth" (3Jn 4). We recently received an invitation to the baptism of a young man who had grown up in the Church. With the invitation, he also thanked us for our contribution to his spiritual journey since he was a young child. What a joy for us to read!

Preaching the Gospel and conversions

When Paul and Barnabas are on their way to Jerusalem, passing through Phoenicia and Samaria, they meet some Christians and tell them about the conversion of Gentiles during their previous trip. This news was a source of joy for their brothers: "This news made all the believers very glad" (Ac 15:3).

A true story

One day when I was waiting for my train at the Gare de Lyon in Paris, I distributed Gospel leaflets throughout the station. Once I was on the train, I continued to give them out in all the carriages. When I got back to my six-seat compartment, I was exhausted. I said to the Lord, "I have done enough work today. I am not going to distribute the leaflets to the five people here because I want to be quiet and have a nap. I did not want to be making conversation all the way to Valence." Another reason for not evangelising in my compartment was that the couple opposite me were blind. Surely it would be silly to give leaflets to people who cannot see?!

The train arrives in the station. Everyone starts getting their bags. To have a clear conscience, I take some leaflets from my pocket and give them to my fellow travellers. Handing the leaflet to the blind couple, I say to them, "You can ask someone to read this to you. My address and phone number are on the back".

Six months later, I receive an astonishing phone call... The blind couple wanted to let me know that, thanks to the leaflet I had given them, they had become Christians, had joined a Church and were soon going to be baptised. What joy!

God wants to use me

For many years, my wife and I have been planting Churches in the south of France. We have gone through difficult times when we have not always seen much fruit for our work; and also moments of great joy when we have seen the Churches grow, spiritually and in number. I think back to the time when we started the Church in Pierrelatte, there were only four of us sitting round a table writing down the constitution, confession of faith and the internal regulations of the future Church. A few months later when the district council at Nyons confirmed the creation of the Church association was official, what joy!

Later, we were able to buy land and construct a beautiful building for the Church, what joy!

We were able to celebrate the inauguration of the Church in the presence of new Christians, our neighbours, the Christians from surrounding Churches, and the Mayor of the town who gave a "polished speech". What joy!

That Church grew and God provided a French Pastoral couple, elders, and a team of potential leaders. Now the Church is autonomous and working without us being there! Can you believe it? What joy!

That joy did not come from what we were able to accomplish for God in that context but, rather, from knowing that God wanted to use us in his plan and that he continues to act, even better, without us.

New Churches in France, a joy!

You will be encouraged to hear that a new Church is planted, on average, every ten days in France: thirty-six a year. Is that not a cause for joy?

Space for reflection: questions and practical application

1. What are the characteristics of authentic joy according to the Bible?

2. Do you know a joyful Christian? What is his influence on you and those around him?

3. What are the sources of joy mentioned in this book? Can you think of any others?

4. How should we understand James 1:2: “Consider it pure joy, my brothers and sisters, whenever you face trials of many kinds”?

5. Nehemiah said: “the joy of the LORD is your strength” (Ne 8:10). How is joy strength? Explain this verse with an example from your own experience.

Meditation and prayer

Come, let us sing for joy to the LORD;
let us shout aloud to the Rock of our salvation.
Let us come before him with thanksgiving
and extol him with music and song.

For the LORD *is the great God,*
the great King above all gods.
In his hand are the depths of the earth,
and the mountain peaks belong to him.
The sea is his, for he made it,
and his hands formed the dry land.

Come, let us bow down in worship,
let us kneel before the LORD *our Maker;*
for he is our God
and we are the people of his pasture,
the flock under his care.

Take time to contemplate this Psalm 95:1-7

MY PRAYER

I want my joy to overflow, my God, because you are my rock, the source of my salvation: you are a great and all-powerful God. I want to express my joy, today, through singing, through music, but also through a positive, grateful and constructive attitude. I recognise that it is not always easy to remain joyful. I need your intervention and the help of your Holy Spirit. I also want to pray that my Church would be an oasis of joy; in the name of Jesus. Amen.

YOUR PRAYER

— Peace —

"But the fruit of the Spirit is love, joy, **peace**, patience, kindness, goodness, faithfulness, gentleness and self-control" (Galatians 5:22)

Every country in the world has its own diplomats. These people are highly educated, often having undertaken advanced studies, and are very well paid. They travel across the world to meet the elite of different countries in luxury hotels; they participate in or organise banquets and all of this in order to establish a dialogue, build trust and keep the peace.

It is essential to have professionals dedicated to maintaining peace, people who know how to manage and cultivate peace in relationships. They listen, negotiate and try to come to agreement in spite of cultural, political, linguistic or historical differences. All of this without offending or angering anyone! It is a real art! Thanks to them, many wars have been prevented.

Although not on such a grand scale, we are, through our words, attitudes and actions, continually building or destroying relationships, promoting peace or war, unity or conflict, harmony or division.

Through our words, attitudes and actions, we are continually building or destroying relationships, promoting peace or war, unity or conflict, harmony or division.

The absence of peace will affect our physical, psychological and even spiritual health. Peace is a powerful weapon which can combat anguish, anxiety and nervousness.

Definition: in Greek, this word suggests serenity, calm and a lack of agitation. In Roman times, the Emperor placed a "guardian of the peace" in every town and village to maintain order.

Now, let's look at the word "peace" in biblical thought. The equivalent word in Hebrew is "Shalom" which means "to be whole". It has become a way of greeting someone: "Shalom!" – "Are you whole?", "Are you doing well physically, psychologically and spiritually?"

In English, we say "How are you?"; a vague and impersonal question which only expects a "fine" or "well" in reply, even if the person is struggling in difficult circumstances. We need to ask more precise questions to know if everything is going well: "How is your health? How is your family? At work? Are you stressed at the moment?..."

I would like to give you two images to understand the meaning of the word "shalom":

1) After the many stages in the construction of a house: foundations, exterior, interior, the owners invite family and friends over for a housewarming. There is a party with cake and champagne! Everything is complete! There is nothing left to add.

2) I am thinking of an old black and white wedding photo, taken on the steps of a large Church: it is a photo of the whole family, grandparents, parents, siblings, uncles, aunts and cousins. The entire family is present and there is no one missing.

"Shalom" is this idea: a whole, complete peace.

A peaceful person is worth their weight in gold: Alex

A peaceful person could perhaps be seen as a weakling or spineless. But to be a peaceful person does not equate to being weak. On the contrary, it requires strength. When I was young, there was a man who made a strong impression on me. I greatly admired this man, whom I am going to call Alex. He was a Christian and a headmaster. He also taught our youth Bible study group at Church. He seemed to know the Bible off by heart.

On several occasions, I attended the Church's yearly business meeting. Alex sometimes led these meetings and, when he was there, everything went well and peacefully. He knew how to respond to quarrelsome people with gentleness and diplomacy and thus kept the peace. When he was absent, things were different. It was often heated!

In the Bible, the word peace does not just mean "absence of conflict", tranquillity, silence or calm. It has a much more profound meaning.

> *"God is not a God of disorder but of peace" (1Cor 14:33).*

It is a peace which finds its source in God

"God is a God of peace", this affirmation appears often in the Bible (Ro 15:33; 16:20; 2Co 13:11; 1Th 5:23; Heb 13:20). One of God's titles is "The Lord is peace" (Jdg 6:24).

"God is not a God of disorder but of peace" (1Co 14:33).

In order to cultivate our relationship with God, others and ourselves, we need peace, a gift from God already in our hearts which we must use.

Why did the apostle Paul often begin his letters to the Churches with this phrase?: "Grace and peace to you from God our Father and the Lord Jesus Christ" (1Co 1:3). Because there were conflicts in the Churches, difficulties, people who did not get on with one another, like Euodia and Syntyche in the Philippian Church (Php 4:2). The apostle Paul invites his readers to live in peace with one another.

This peace within the Church comes from the spiritual authority instituted by God. The elders, and deacons are there, along with others, to keep order and peace.

Order is established, and peace re-established through **teaching**, as Paul did in his epistles, through **visits** intended to encourage, console or warn those who have lost their peace for some reason; by **discerning the different gifts** which people have and encouraging them to serve the Church.

When a person is not in the right place in the Church, it creates problems.

An unpleasant memory springs to mind thinking of this subject: it did not take place in Church but during an evangelical youth convention, Mission 83 in Lausanne. Around 10,000 young people were expected to attend. The organising committee had entrusted me with the responsibility of training the leaders for the small group discussions. I was proud to wear my badge saying: "Trainer for discussion group leaders". The first day of the convention arrived. I was wandering through the various offices greeting my friends; I went to the welcome area and looked at the long queue of participants, hoping that I would recognise someone. The problem was I had left my post. The welcome team were sending the discussion group leaders to my office but I was not there. They needed information from me regarding the timetable, locations, materials for the group discussions but Ian was absent.

The convention director was informed and came looking for me. He took me back to my office himself, sat me down and said: "You are going to stay here, at your post, and get on with your own job rather than trying to do someone else's!"

I never forgot that warning. That reprimand got me back on track. When we are in the right place, using the gifts that the Lord has given us, order reigns and we promote peace. On the other hand, if we are not in the correct place, chaos ensues and everyone is affected by it. Paul encourages Christians to stick close to their ministry and not to err (Ro 12:6-8).

Only one thing is worse than a person who thinks he has no gift: a person who thinks they have a gift which they do not possess!

It is a peace centred on Jesus

Jesus is called "Prince of Peace" (Isa 9:6).

> *"For he himself is our peace, who has made the two one and has destroyed the barrier" (Eph 2:14).*

> "For he himself is our peace, who has made the two one and has destroyed the barrier, the dividing wall of hostility, by setting aside in his flesh the law with its commands and regulations. His purpose was to create in himself one new humanity out of the two, thus making peace, and in one body to reconcile both of them to God through the cross, by which he put to death their hostility. He came and preached peace to you who were far away and peace to those who were near. For through him we both have access to the Father by one Spirit" (Eph 2:14-18).

Characteristics of this peace

It is powerful

We are told in Ephesians 2:14 that Jesus is our peace, **he has destroyed the barrier**.

We struggle to imagine that peace can destroy and change situations!

And yet it is a power which, in this context, removes the hate and lack of understanding between Jews and Gentiles, re-establishing a relationship between them and with God.

By his flesh, his sacrifice on the cross, Jesus made the sacrifices of the Old Testament obsolete in order to create new men through him, whatever their origin.

"Therefore, if anyone is in Christ, he is a new creation" (2Co 5:17).

What power!

Jesus' peace makes a new creation, a new birth called "conversion", possible.

I recommend Josh McDowell's book: *More than a carpenter.*[24] He gives the testimonies of very different people: a scientist, an IT expert, a police officer, a prostitute, a thief, a government minister, a cow-boy, a professional golfer, a doctor, a farmer, a senator, a gang leader, a philosopher, an architect, a prisoner, atheists and people from different continents, cultures and religions whose lives have been transformed by Jesus' peace in their hearts.

Peace I leave with you; my peace I give you. I do not give to you as the world gives. Do not let your hearts be troubled and do not be afraid" (Jn 14:27).

It is also **God's peace** which resurrected Jesus:

"May the God of peace, who through the blood of the eternal covenant brought back from the dead the Lord Jesus..." (Heb 13:20).

It is **the peace of God** which is going to secure the final victory over Satan:

"The God of peace will soon crush Satan under your feet. The grace of our Lord Jesus be with you" (Ro 16:20).

It is available

"Peace I leave with you; my peace I give you. I do not give to you as the world gives. Do not let your hearts be troubled and do not be afraid" (Jn 14:27).

How can we access this peace?

Through repentance

Many of us have access to the internet at home and it is great... when it works! It is so frustrating when it does not work. When we are out and about and staying at a hotel, the first question we ask is often: “Is there internet access?” We always want to be connected to stay in contact with friends, family or work.

The Bible tells us that our “connection” with God was broken because of sin.

“But your iniquities have separated you from your God; your sins have hidden his face from you, so that he will not hear” (Isa 59:2).

The apostle Paul calls us to be reconciled with God: “We implore you on Christ’s behalf: be reconciled to God” (2Co 5:20). This can only be done through Jesus. He carried our sins on the cross so that we would have the chance to be reconciled to God and make peace with him. God made the first move. It is up to us to acknowledge and confess our sin so that we can enter into an intimate relationship with him and, this way, have peace in our hearts.

“Therefore, since we have been justified through faith, we have peace with God through our Lord Jesus Christ” (Ro 5:1).

Then, if we do sin, we can always come back to God and ask his forgiveness to find peace again.

If you would like to become a Christian, ask forgiveness for your sins, invite Jesus into your heart and he will give you peace. If you are a Christian, and you need peace, stop and ask God to pour his peace into your heart now.

Through requests

Through prayer, we can bring all our worries and needs to God.

“Do not be anxious about anything, but in every situation, by prayer and petition, with thanksgiving, present your requests to God” (Php 4:6).

“And the peace of God, which transcends all understanding, will guard your hearts and your minds in Christ Jesus” (Php 4:7).

When we place our worries and needs before God:

- God fills our hearts with his peace

- This peace guards and protects our heart – The word guard comes from the Greek word "parousía". It is a military term which refers to the extreme vigilance of an army marching around a city to protect it. God's peace will protect our whole personality: our intelligence, our will, our emotions. What a beautiful promise!
- This peace guards our thoughts

Through an act of the will

"Blessed are the peacemakers" (Mt 5:9).

"Let us therefore make every effort to do what leads to peace and to mutual edification" (Ro 14:19).

"Make every effort to live in peace" (Heb 12:14).

"If you want to enjoy life and wish to see good times [...] you must strive for peace with all your heart" (1Pe 3:10-11, GNT).

I would like to encourage you to consider ways to make or restore peace. Perhaps you are angry with someone and the relationship is difficult or at a complete standstill. I would like to urge you to take the first step and ask for forgiveness: "If it is possible, as far as it depends on you, live at peace with everyone" (Ro 12:18).

When a situation is tense in Church, be a peacemaker. Our responsibility is threefold: possess this peace, maintain it and pass it on to others.

I have a talent for creating stress and sometimes even conflict wherever I go. My wife often says: "Ian could stress out a Buddha!" Procuring peace and harmony is not something which comes easily to me. This makes me think of a time when I was planning a purchase. Sharing my intentions with my friends, I realised that it was going to create tensions. To re-establish peace, I made the painful decision not to go ahead with the purchase. This decision brought peace into my heart and produced harmonious relationships with my friends. We need to ask God for wisdom in our situations of conflict so that we make the correct decisions that will procure unity and peace with others. Often, I have had to learn to "eat my words"! Not easy, I must admit.

Spreading peace with the Gospel

"How beautiful on the mountains are the feet of those who bring good news, who proclaim peace!" (Isa 52:7).

The message of the Gospel, received in people's hearts, brings peace.

On a trip to Thailand to visit and encourage missionary friends of ours, we went with them to visit a Buddhist monastery for female priests. These women lived in huts in the forest which surrounded the temple. Some of them came from western countries.

> *"How beautiful on the mountains are the feet of those who bring good news, who proclaim peace!" (Isa 52:7).*

They were there to seek inner peace through meditation, fasting, yoga etc. We were able to speak with a German girl who spoke good English: Ursula. Like all the other female priests, her head and eyebrows were shaved and she wore a long white robe. The meeting was very interesting: we were curious to know what had brought her there, to live in complete deprivation. She admitted to us that nothing in the West had given her the sense of peace she longed for. Having asked whether she had managed to find it here, she told us that she was still searching for it. As we were leaving, we left her a Bible and our missionary friends promised to go back and visit her.

Three years later, when I was a pastor in Vevey in Switzerland, I was told after a service that a young woman wanted to speak to me. It was Ursula. I did not recognise her at first because she had grown her hair and was in western dress. She told me that, thanks to reading the gospel and being supported by our missionary friends, she had become a Christian and had found profound peace in Jesus.

Praying for peace in the Church

Paul said this prayer for Christians in Rome: "May the God of hope fill you with all joy and peace as you trust in him, so that you may overflow with hope by the power of the Holy Spirit" (Ro 15:13).

Praying for peace in the world

We are invited to intercede for the leaders of our world "that we may live a quiet and peaceful life" (1Ti 2:1-2).

Space for reflection: questions and practical application

1. Are you experiencing God's peace just now? If not, ask him to fill you with his peace right now.

2. According to Philippians 4:6-7, what happens when we bring our needs and/or worries to God in prayer?

3. The apostle Paul invites us to live in peace with one another, "If it is possible, as far as it depends on you, live at peace with everyone" (Ro 12:18). How should we understand this verse?

4. Do you want to work for peace in your family, Church or workplace? What could you do to achieve this in concrete terms?

5. Do you want to bear witness to your faith to those around you and give them access to the peace which only Jesus can give?

Reflection and prayer

Lord, make me an instrument of your peace;
where there is hatred, let me sow love;
where there is injury, pardon;
where there is doubt, faith;
where there is despair, hope;
where there is darkness, light;
and where there is sadness, joy.

O Divine Master,
grant that I may not so much seek
to be consoled as to console;
to be understood, as to understand;
to be loved, as to love;
for it is in giving that we receive,
it is in pardoning that we are pardoned,
and it is in dying that we are born to Eternal Life.
Amen.
(Prayer of St Francis of Assisi[25])

MY PRAYER

Lord, it is easier for me to tear down and criticise than to build up and bless. Come to my aid and, through my words and acts, make me an agent, an instrument of your peace in my family, in my Church… In the name of Jesus. Amen.

YOUR PRAYER

— Patience —

"But the fruit of the Spirit is love, joy, peace, **patience**, kindness, goodness, faithfulness, gentleness and self-control" (Galatians 5:22)

We are now looking at the second group of fruits: patience, goodness and kindness, which relate to our relationship with others.

Definition in the dictionary: the quality of being patient, as the bearing of provocation, annoyance, misfortune, or pain, without complaint, loss of temper, irritation, or the like.

Do you need patience? I have to admit it is not one of my strong points. I need patience to be able to persevere when I do not see visible results in my ministry; to put up with others; to wait for answers to my prayers; to go through difficult times…

There is a Dutch proverb which says: "A handful of patience is worth more than a bushel of brain!" Here is another quotation from the same book: "Patience is a tree with bitter roots but sweet fruits".[26]

There is a Dutch proverb which says: "A handful of patience is worth more than a bushel of brain!"

I heard of a Christian who prayed with sincerity: "Lord give me patience, but right now!"

Definition in the Bible

In biblical thought, **perseverance** and **patience** are twin sisters. It is difficult to separate them. These two words have the same root in Greek. They describe the unwavering attitude of someone who does not give in.

In the New Testament, these words "perseverance" and "patience" are often mentioned in relation to moments of trial and tribulation.

"We also glory in our sufferings, because we know that suffering produces perseverance; perseverance, character; and character, hope" (Ro 5:3-4).

"Therefore, among God's Churches we boast about your perseverance and faith in all the persecutions and trials you are enduring" (2Th 1:4).

God is patient. Patience is one of God's great characteristics.

God's patience is always accompanied by his goodness.

"But they, our ancestors, became arrogant [...] But you are a forgiving God, gracious and compassionate, slow to anger and abounding in love" (Ne 9:16-17). In the same chapter in Nehemiah, the Levites pray to God in which they list everything he has done for his people: he gave life to his creation (v.6), he chose Abraham and promised him land (v.7-8), he sent signs and wonders (v.10), he showed his glory (v.10), he guided them (v.12), he gave them excellent commandments (v.13), he gave them bread and water (v.15) and he gave them land (v.15).

God is particularly patient and good with the people of Israel who, later, turn their back on him: "They refused to listen and failed to remember the miracles you performed among them" (Ne 9:17).

"And the same is true of what God has done. He wanted to show his anger and to make his power known. But he was very patient in enduring those who were the objects of his anger, who were doomed to destruction" (Ro 9:22, GNT).

What is the aim of God's patience? It is to make people repent: "do you show contempt for the riches of his kindness, forbearance and patience, not realizing that God's kindness is intended to lead you to repentance?" (Ro 2:4).

Notice the difference between man's heart and God's heart in Nehemiah 9:

Man's heart		God's heart
Arrogant (v. 16)	→	Compassionate (v. 17)
Stiff-necked (v. 16)	→	Slow to anger (v. 17)
Disobedient (v. 16)	→	Patient (v. 30)
Refused to listen (v. 17)	→	Listens (v. 9)
Forgetful (v. 17)	→	Does not forget (v. 32)
Rebellious (v. 17)	→	Righteous (v. 8)
Idolatrous (v. 18)	→	Faithful (v. 33)
Blasphemous (v. 18)	→	Guiding (v. 12)

What is God's reaction?

What is the aim of God's patience? It is to make people repent.

"But you are a forgiving God, gracious and compassionate, slow to anger and abounding in love. Therefore, you did not desert them, even when they cast for themselves an image of a calf and said, 'This is your god, who brought you up out of Egypt,' or when they committed awful blasphemies. Because of your great compassion you did not abandon them in the wilderness" (Ne 9:17-19).

In a hostile atmosphere of rebellion and disobedience, God is patient and slow to anger. He could have intervened in a radical and thunderous way, it would have been justified, but he chooses to wait… He stays his hand. What patience!

The patience of Jesus Christ

The patience of Jesus is exemplary. The believer is invited to:

"Surrounded then as we are by these serried ranks of witnesses, let us strip off everything that hinders us, as well as the sin which dogs our feet, and let us run the race that we have to run with patience, our eyes fixed on Jesus the source and the goal of our faith. For he himself endured a cross and thought nothing of its shame because of the joy he knew would follow his suffering; and he is now seated at the right hand of God's throne. Think constantly of him enduring all that sinful men could say against him and you will not lose your purpose or your courage" (Heb 12:1-3, J.B. Phillips).

Without the help of the Holy Spirit, I cannot exercise restraint or patience. I must humbly admit that when faced with critics or hurtful words my natural reaction is to return evil for evil, to take revenge. I have often had to cry out to God to help me not to do or say anything and to leave it to him. If, in your heart, you feel resentment towards someone who has wronged you, ask God in prayer to remove any bitterness from your heart, and help you to exercise self-restraint and allow him to act.

The first dimension of the word patience is **our ability to break or halt an action that would cause suffering**.

John Chrysostom defined patience as "the ability to not exercise vengeance". For Lightfoot, it involves "not retaliating against someone who has wronged us".

The word patience (or forbearance) is often described as "long-suffering": that is, being able to wait in spite of the suffering caused by renouncing vengeance. Jesus is the perfect example of this: "When they hurled their insults at him, he did not retaliate; when he suffered, he made no threats. Instead, he entrusted himself to him who judges justly" (1Pe 2:23).

Impatient people are weak. Patience, on the other hand, is the sign of an inner strength and the capacity to endure without complaint.

Being patient means knowing that God is preparing something better for us, in spite of the setbacks and annoyances.

The second dimension is **our ability to keep going, remain faithful and maintain our enthusiasm in spite of opposition and trials**.

We often lack perseverance and tenacity, don't we? We start something and then we put it aside: whether it is a book, knitting, a sport or a musical instrument.

In Numbers 12.3, we are told that Moses "was a very humble man, more humble than anyone else on the face of the earth". In the French Bible it is translated: "Moïse était un homme fort patient," "extremely patient".

Moses was chosen by God to lead his people undoubtedly because of his humility, meekness and patience. The people of Israel were often rebellious. Moses had to cope with their complaints and stubbornness for over 40 years.

The epistles of the New Testament urge perseverance:

"The only thing that counts is faith expressing itself through love. You were running a good race. Who cut in on you to keep you from obeying the truth?" (Gal 5:6-7).

"You need to persevere" (Heb 10:36).

We recently decided, as a couple, to pray every day at lunchtime for one of the fifty countries in which Christians are persecuted. It lasted a week and then we gave up… We lacked perseverance!

When activities at the Church began again in September, lots of people signed up to do the cleaning, or made the resolution to attend the weekly meetings etc. By February, the list of cleaning volunteers was almost empty and few people were attending the Bible study and prayer meetings. All because of a lack of perseverance!

And what about perseverance in difficult times?

To persevere in times of trial, we need real motivation. We can find it in Paul's letter to the Romans:

"Therefore, since we have been justified through faith, we have **peace** with God through our Lord Jesus Christ, through whom we have gained access by faith into this grace in which we now stand. And we boast in the hope of the glory of God. Not only so, but we also glory in our sufferings, because we know that suffering produces **perseverance**; perseverance, character; and character, hope. And hope does not put us to shame, because God's **love** has been poured out into our hearts through the Holy Spirit, who has been given to us" (Ro 5:1-5).

This tree bears fruit: love, joy, peace... What determines the quality of the fruit is not the trunk but the roots. Notice that this tree's roots are plunged into the "soil of suffering and trials ". In the Bible, persevering does not mean waiting without saying or doing anything; on the contrary, it involves confronting the realities of life and "sparks off" a process towards maturity and hope.

It is when we go through difficult times that we often realise that we need God's intervention and that, without him, we cannot do anything.

In the text above, Romans 5:3, there is a very important word: "know". This means that every time we face trials, there are lessons that we can learn from them. Times of trial teach us:

- To be patient
- To carry our burdens without making a fuss
- To reinforce and develop our strength of character
- To put even more trust in God
- To make our faith and hope strong and unwavering

Notice that there are three of the fruits of the Spirit mentioned in this passage: **peace** (v.1), God's **love** poured into our hearts (v.5) and **patience** or **perseverance**, which produce character and hope (v.5).

James, speaking about trials in his epistle, goes even further: "Consider it **pure joy**, my brothers and sisters, whenever you face trials of many kinds, because you know that the testing of your faith produces perseverance" (Jas 1:2-3).

The picture is complete: we have love, joy, peace, patience, character and hope. This perseverance is often linked to a goal, a noble and glorious perspective.

"The man who patiently endures the temptations and trials that come to him is the truly happy man. For once his testing is complete he will receive the crown of life which the Lord has promised to all who love him" (Jas1:12, J.B. Phillips).

"Be patient, then, brothers and sisters, until the Lord's coming" (Jas 5:7).

"…let us throw off everything that hinders and the sin that so easily entangles. And let us run with perseverance the race marked out for us, fixing our eyes on Jesus, the pioneer and perfecter of faith. For the joy set before him he endured the cross, scorning its shame, and sat down at the right hand of the throne of God" (Heb 12:1-2).

Patience in practice

In sickness, mourning and other trials, let's keep our eyes on Jesus and the hope of eternal life with him.

John Knox, a Scottish reformer, said "trials and difficulties are the 'spurs' used by God to propel us into a richer and more profound life of dependence and prayer." God sometimes shows us our limits so that we will depend on the power of his Spirit and learn to be more patient and persevering.

> *"Trials and difficulties are the 'spurs' used by God to propel us into a richer and more profound life of dependence and prayer."* John Knox

I used to have an old bike which an elderly lady gave me. Every time the road started to climb, I had to get off the bike and walk, until it was flat or downhill again. A friend recently gave me a great bike which he was no longer using: an all-terrain bike with twelve gears. It is great on flat roads and also uphill! Thanks to a little button on the handlebars, I can shift gears and I am laughing all the way!

You understand. We need to accept that there are some problems which we are not strong enough to tackle ourselves. We need access to the gears of the Spirit to continue moving forwards, with patience and perseverance.

Patience is essential for creating unity in the Church

For Paul, patience is the sign of authentic Christian service.

"As a prisoner for the Lord, then, I urge you to live a life worthy of the calling you have received. Be completely humble and gentle; be patient, bearing with one another in love. Make every effort to keep the unity of the Spirit through the bond of peace" (Eph 4:1-3).

"Love is **patient**, love is kind. It does not envy, it does not boast, it is not proud [...] It always protects, always trusts, always hopes, always perseveres" (1Co 13:4,7).

This quality is essential for leaders in the Church: the servant "must be kind to all, ready and able to teach: he must have **patience** and the ability gently to correct those who oppose his message" (2Ti 2:24-25, J.B. Phillips).

Perseverance is required to grow and make progress in our faith

The growth of the Church was directly linked to the perseverance of the first Christians: "They continued steadily [persevered] learning the **teaching** of the apostles, and joined in their **fellowship**, in the **breaking of bread**, and in **prayer**" (Ac 2:42, J.B. Phillips). Notice that they were doing all these things in the context of opposition and fierce persecution. In spite of that, they were able to persevere and keep their enthusiasm.

Patience and perseverance encourage others!

When we persevere in difficult, indeed impossible, situations, we are an example to our brothers and sisters around us and this encourages them. Never underestimate the impact that your life can have on others.

The people who encourage us the most are not necessarily great preachers or leaders in the Church. Rather, they are the people who always trust in God's Word and who we see persevere day after day, whatever the circumstances, in their walk with the Lord. Let's imitate them and be role models for others, particularly young people. Our love, joy and patience will help them to become attached to the Church, to love it and become involved.

George Müller, a great man of faith in the nineteenth century, prayed every day for the conversion of five friends. After eighteen months of prayer, one of them became a Christian. After five years of intercession, the second accepted Christ into his life. After six years, the third took the same step. Shortly before his death, his fourth friend gave his life to the Lord. George Müller did not see the answer to the prayer which he had continued to say on behalf of his fifth friend. Only a few years after his death, his fifth friend gave his life to Jesus. What a beautiful example of perseverance in prayer, which we are encouraged to follow.[27]

I am thinking of a dear Christian friend, Jonathan McRostie, now with the Lord. He was the head of Operation Mobilisation in Europe. He was a humble and joyful man with a fervent faith in God. After a car accident, he was left tetraplegic and in a wheelchair. In spite of this serious handicap, and constant suffering, he kept his passion for God for over thirty years and persevered till the end. What an example for me!

Space for reflection: questions and practical application

1. In your own words, define the word "patience".

2. What makes you impatient in everyday life?

3. In Acts 2:42, four areas in which we should exercise patience and perseverance are mentioned. What are your strong and weak points within these four areas?

4. Have you ever felt encouraged by the patience and perseverance of someone you know? Take time to thank them.

MY PRAYER

My God, thank you for your patience towards me. I have sometimes lived as though you did not exist. I did not pray and I neglected your Word. But you have always been there, present and watching over me, like a father who never abandons his children. What great patience! I think of the verse which says: "All day long I have held out my hands to an obstinate people" (Isa 65:2). Thank you for your out-stretched hand, full of love, grace and mercy.

Lord, I want to ask your forgiveness for all the times I have become annoyed, or angry with a brother or sister in Christ. I lack patience, I realise this. I have also been impatient with you, Lord, when I have not seen quick answers to my prayers, or results in the time I expected. Looking back, I understood that your timing was perfect.

I pray all this in Jesus' name. Amen.

YOUR PRAYER

— Kindness and Goodness —

> "But the fruit of the Spirit is love, joy, peace, patience, **kindness**, **goodness**, faithfulness, gentleness and self-control" (Galatians 5:22)

Kindness and goodness are part of the same family. That is why we will look at the two together. It is a little difficult to distinguish between the two at times. Nonetheless, I would like to share the nuances of these words with you.

These two qualities are brought together in Romans 15:14:

"For myself I feel certain that you, my brothers, have real **Christian character and experience** [goodness], and that you are capable of **keeping each other on the right road** [kindness]" (J.B. Phillips).

Goodness can be said to refer to the good inner attitudes we have which foster, facilitate and lead to kindness. It is an attitude which can take different forms: listening, a prayer, a thought or an attitude. In Latin, goodness is "bonitas", which can be translated by "good character". A good person has a positive attitude towards those around them. He does not look for evil in others and encourages them in the right path.

These good inner attitudes, this goodness, inevitably express themselves through kind actions.

> *Goodness can be said to refer to the good inner attitudes we have which foster, facilitate and lead to kindness.*

Kindness is the concrete expression of goodness, accompanied by the pleasure of making others happy. It is goodness incarnate.

In Hebrew, kindness is a pleasant action which gives the other person deep satisfaction. In the New Testament, it is a good fruit or good works. Someone who shows kindness is an agent of good, they have a serving heart.

"Kindness is a language that the deaf can hear and the blind can see."[28]

God is good

All through the Old Testament we see God's kindness towards his creation, man in particular.

"The LORD is good to all; he has compassion on all he has made" (Ps 145:9).

"For the LORD is good and his love endures forever; his faithfulness continues through all generations" (Ps 100:5).

"Surely God is good to Israel" (Ps 73:1).

"… according to your love remember me, for you, Lord, are good. Good and upright is the Lord; therefore he instructs sinners in his ways. He guides the humble in what is right and teaches them his way" (Ps 25:7-9).

God's goodness is…

Great, immense

"How abundant are the good things that you have stored up for those who fear you" (Ps 31:19).

"Answer me, LORD, out of the goodness of your love; in your great mercy turn to me" (Ps 69:16).

"Your lovingkindness, O LORD, extends to the heavens" (Ps 36:5, NASB).

Eternal

“But for those who honour the LORD, his love lasts forever, and his goodness endures for all generations” (Ps 103:15, GNT).

> *“How abundant are the good things that you have stored up for those who fear you” (Ps 31:19).*

“But the lovingkindness of the LORD is from everlasting to everlasting on those who fear Him” (Ps 103:17, NASB).

Everywhere

“He loves righteousness and justice; The earth is full of the lovingkindness of the LORD” (Ps 33:5, NASB).

Constant

“The LORD’s lovingkindnesses indeed never cease [...] They are new every morning” (La 3:22-23, NASB).

Priceless

“Because Your lovingkindness is better than life” (Ps 63:3, NASB).

A support

“If I should say, “My foot has slipped,” your lovingkindness, O LORD, will hold me up” (Ps 94:18, NASB).

We are urged to come and discover this goodness of God, and reflect on it.

“Taste and see that the LORD is good; blessed is the one who takes refuge in him” (Ps 34:8).

In the New Testament, God continues to give generously: his son (Jn 3:16), his Spirit (Jn 14:17), his Word (2Ti 3:16), his Church (1Ti 3:5, 15), gifts (1Co 12:4-11), ministries (Eph 4:11-12) etc.

Jesus' exceptional kindness

Throughout his ministry, Jesus shows real kindness towards the sick, the poor, and children… and often in situations of conflict, indifference and unbelief.

"… do good to them, and lend to them without expecting to get anything back. Then your reward will be great" (Lk 6:35).

How should we react to this divine kindness?

Praise and thanks

God shows his great kindness to us even though we do not deserve it. God's mercy is a lifeline for us in our wretchedness! And when we realise that such a great God came to save us, sinful and insignificant as we are, we can only "fall on our knees" to praise and thank him. "The Lord is gracious and compassionate, slow to anger and rich in love. The Lord is good to all; he has compassion on all he has made. All your works praise you, Lord; your faithful people extol you" (Ps 145:8-10).

When I am feeling discouraged, I sometimes take a blank piece of paper and, on one side, I write down some of God's attributes and, on the other, I write down everything he has done for me. I can testify to the fact that this puts what is getting me down into perspective and encourages me to praise and thank my God who is full of kindness.

God's mercy is a lifeline for us in our wretchedness!

I would make a slight difference between praising God and thanking him. I exalt God for who he is and for his attributes. Then, I thank him for all that he has done for me.

Repentance

In Romans 2:4, the apostle Paul speaks about a judgement for those who hold God's kindness in contempt: "Or do you show contempt for the riches of his kindness, forbearance and patience, not realizing that God's kindness is intended to lead you to repentance?" (Ro 2:4). The phrase "show contempt" may seem a bit strong to us, but we have to admit that we often easily forget what God has done for us. I call it "spiritual Alzheimer's".

Let's confess that we have often forgotten, and therefore shown contempt for, God's goodness.

Showing kindness to others

"Actions speak louder than words, but, with God, motives speak louder than either."[29]

When I understand that I am the object of God's kindness, I can, in turn, reflect that around me. The Word of God urges us to do "good works".

This is what Paul did when he wrote to Titus: "But when the kindness and love of God our Saviour appeared, he saved us, not because of righteous things we had done, but because of his mercy [...] And I want you to stress these things, so that those who have trusted in God may be careful to devote themselves to doing what is good" (Tit 3:4, 8).

He also wrote to the Colossians: "Therefore, as God's chosen people, holy and dearly loved, clothe yourselves with compassion, kindness, humility, gentleness and patience. Bear with each other and forgive one another if any of you has a grievance against someone. Forgive as the Lord forgave you" (Col 3:12-13).

Here are some examples of people in the Bible who knew how to clothe themselves in kindness.

* *Joseph – Genesis 45*

Joseph's brothers, jealous of him, want to kill him but then decide to sell him to traders going to Egypt. Joseph is imprisoned there but he is then pardoned by Pharaoh, who also gives him an important position in the country. Joseph finds himself face to face with his brothers who have come to ask for food. What is Joseph's reaction?

Kindness is often "contagious"

"You intended to harm me, but God intended it for good [...] So then, don't be afraid. I will provide for you and your children." And he reassured them and spoke kindly to them" (Ge 50:20-21).

The kindness which Joseph shows his brothers touches Pharaoh who, in turn, is generous to them:

"When the news reached Pharaoh's palace that Joseph's brothers had come, Pharaoh and all his officials were pleased" (Ge 45:16).

"...bring your father and your families back to me. I will give you the best of the land of Egypt and you can enjoy the fat of the land'" (Ge 45:18).

Kindness is often "contagious".

* *David – 2 Samuel 9:13*

Mephibosheth was the son of Jonathan, David's friend, and the grandson of King Saul. After the death of these two, Mephibosheth, who was lame in both feet, was certainly trying to keep a low profile, fearing that David would retaliate against him.

David calls for him and tells him: "Don't be afraid, for I will surely show you kindness for the sake of your father Jonathan" (2Sa 9:7).

David returns all of the lands which belonged to Saul to Mephibosheth and invites him to eat at his table for the rest of his life.

* *The Good Samaritan – Luke 10:25-37*

The story of the Good Samaritan is a parable told by Jesus. The character is fictitious but serves to convey the message that it is important to love our neighbours and demonstrate this through actions.

A man, the victim of robbers, is lying seriously injured on the road. Two religious men arrive one after the other and pass by on the other side of the road.

"But a Samaritan, as he travelled, came where the man was; and when he saw him, he took pity on him. He went to him and bandaged his wounds, pouring on oil and wine. Then he put the man on his own donkey, brought him to an inn and took care of him. The next day he took out two denarii and gave them to the innkeeper. 'Look after him,' he said, 'and when I return, I will reimburse you for any extra expense you may have" (Lk 10:33-35).

What a story! It is important to know that the Samaritans were not well thought of in Israel. The Jews disliked them. And in spite of everything, this man comes to the aid of his neighbour; he looks after him, takes him to the town and pays for the hotel and doctor. Did you notice the expression used in the text: "the Samaritan was moved by compassion"?

The pity which moves the Samaritan to give up his own time, money and effort to help his neighbour reminds us of the compassion which Jesus feels when he sees the crowd: "he had compassion on them" (Mt 9:36). This led him to pray for them, to touch and heal the sick, to cry with his friends and to die on the cross.

In our Western world, we are very preoccupied with ourselves and our own fulfilment. This attitude also works its way into our Churches. We need to ask God, in prayer, for this compassion for our neighbours: compassion to help them with their physical and material needs, and also with their spiritual needs. Many of our fellow citizens today are lost and do not know God. This compassion, sown in our hearts, will put us in the right frame of mind (goodness) to act (kindness).

** Lydia – Acts 16:14-15*

"One of those listening was a woman from the city of Thyatira named Lydia, a dealer in purple cloth. She was a worshiper of God.

The Lord opened her heart to respond to Paul's message. When she and the members of her household were baptized, she invited us to her home. "If you consider me a believer in the Lord," she said, "come and stay at my house." And she persuaded us."

Lydia is the first European to be converted. She shows kindness to Paul and Silas through her hospitality and, without realising it, she is also opening up the door to the evangelisation of Europe.

When I demonstrate goodness through an act of kindness or generosity, I affirm that I was made in the image of a God, who is fundamentally good, and that I was recreated through a new birth to develop this fruit with the help of the Holy Spirit.

> *"Live such good lives among the pagans that [...] they may see your good deeds and glorify God on the day he visits us" (1 Pe 2:12).*

In Acts 11:24, Barnabas is said to be: "a good man, full of the Holy Spirit and faith, and a great number of people were brought to the Lord" (Ac 11:24).

When I show kindness to those around me, it is a powerful testimony!

"You are the light of the world [...]let your light shine before others, that they may see your good deeds and glorify your Father in heaven" (Mt 5:14,16).

"Live such good lives among the pagans that [...] they may see your good deeds and glorify God on the day he visits us" (1Pe 2:12).

William Booth, the founder of the Salvation Army (1829 – 1912) is a wonderful example of goodness and kindness. He worked relentlessly for fifty years to help save people living in poverty. During his last speech in front of seven thousand people in London, he sounded this "War Cry" (name of the Salvation Army's newspaper): "While women weep, as they do now, I'll fight. While little children go hungry, as they do now, I'll fight. While men go to prison, in and out, as they do now, I'll fight. While there is a drunkard left, While there is a poor lost girl upon the streets, While there remains one dark soul without the light of God, I'll fight-I'll fight to the very end!" William Booth died on his knees in prayer. His life can be summarised like this: kindness incarnate which never ceased to give, give, give…

My father-in-law: a gentleman and an agent of God's kindness

Each time I visited my father-in-law, who has now passed away, I always came away with a little gift from him: paper for my photocopier, a pot of jam, fruit etc. There was one time when he had nothing to hand to give me – he accompanied me to the door and suddenly said "Wait! I have forgotten something." I saw him take three beautiful flowers from his own garden and he handed them to me saying: "These are for your wife!" I never left his house without something in my hands.

Practicing kindness often has a "boomerang" effect: "A generous person will prosper; whoever refreshes others will be refreshed" (Pr 11:25).

Practicing kindness often has a "boomerang" effect: "A generous person will prosper; whoever refreshes others will be refreshed" (Pr 11:25). We are not called to be kind to others in order to benefit from it ourselves, but our selfless gestures are a source of joy.

I would like to finish with a quotation from John Wesley[30] (an evangelist and founder of the Methodist Church) about kindness and which gives us a good illustration of the golden rule: "do to others what you would have them do to you" (Mt 7:12).

"Do all the good you can. By all the means you can.
In all the ways you can. In all the places you can.
At all the times you can. To all the people you can.
As long as ever you can." *John Wesley*

Space for reflection: questions and practical application

1. What is the difference between goodness and kindness?

2. Re-read 2 Samuel 9:1-13 about David's kindness to Mephibosheth. What motivated his kindness (9.3)?

3. What does a gesture of kindness produce in us?

4. Lamentations 3:22-23 tells us "the Lord's great love we are not consumed, for his compassions never fail. They are new every morning". What does this mean for us on a daily basis?

Let us spend some time in silence, asking the Lord to sow a new compassion for others in our hearts, good inner attitudes so that we can listen to our neighbour, pray for him and serve him.

MY PRAYER

Lord, give me good inner attitudes (humility, compassion, the ability to listen...) which will encourage me to want what is good for ... (someone).

Help me to express kindness through a concrete gesture to someone in need this week. I ask this of you in Jesus name, Amen.

YOUR PRAYER

— Faithfulness —

> "But the fruit of the Spirit is love, joy, peace, patience, kindness, goodness, **faithfulness**, gentleness and self-control" (Galatians 5:22)

According to translations, this fruit is translated as "faithfulness" or "faith". Faithfulness in Hebrew means "be firm, hold firm"; and "be full of trust" in Greek. Faithfulness refers to feelings towards someone which remain constant.

The theme of faithfulness has an important place in the Word of God.

> *Faithfulness in Hebrew means "be firm, hold firm".*

Notice that there is a difference between faith (trusting in God) and the "gift of faith": "Truly I tell you, if you have faith as small as a mustard seed, you can say to this mountain, 'Move from here to there,' and it will move. Nothing will be impossible for you." This work will not deal with the theme of the "gift of faith".

God is faithful: the consequences for us

- Faithfulness is an attribute of God: "he is the faithful God" (Dt 7:9).
- God keeps his Word: "he who promised is faithful" (Heb 10:23), and his relationships with men are founded on this truth
- His pardon: "he is faithful and just and will forgive us our sins" (1Jn 1:9).

- His protection: "his faithfulness will be your shield" (Ps 91:4).
- His protection during temptation: "God is faithful; he will not let you be tempted[b] beyond what you can bear"; "the Lord is faithful, and he will strengthen you and protect you from the evil one" (2Th 3:3).
- He listens to and answers my prayers: "in your faithfulness and righteousness come to my relief" (Ps 143:1).
- God's faithfulness is limitless: "Your righteousness is like the highest mountains" (Ps 36:6).

The great covenants between God and his people, throughout the Bible, are based on God's faithfulness. Throughout Israel's history, God always remained faithful to his Word in spite of everything. That did not stop his people from being unfaithful and fickle. "if we are faithless, he remains faithful" (2Ti 2:13).

God's faithfulness guarantees us protection during temptation: "God is faithful; he will not let you be tempted beyond what you can bear. But when you are tempted, he will also provide a way out so that you can endure it" (1Co 10:13).

The great covenants between God and his people, throughout the Bible, are based on God's faithfulness.

This divine characteristic encourages and inspires us who believe, and God looks for our faithfulness in return.

In the Bible, there is an impressive list of men and women who are faithful to the Lord: Abraham (Gal 3:9), Moses (Heb 3:5), Paul (1Co 7:25), Lydia (Ac 16:15), Timothy (1Co 4:17), Tychicus (Eph 6:21), Onesimus (Col 4:9), Silas (1Pe 5:12), Antipas (Rev 2:13)…

The source of faith – the Word

Faithfulness is closely linked to faith. Faith is our ability to trust God's Word: "faith comes from hearing the message, and the message is heard through the word about Christ" (Ro 10:17). It is therefore important to engage with and root ourselves thoroughly in the Word of God. God's promises are greater than life's problems.

Archimedes said: "Give me a lever and a place to stand and I will move the earth." Stand on the promises of the Word of God and they will act as a lever to your faith.

God's faithfulness assures us protection during temptation.

Faith – one of Jesus' concerns

Jesus prays that the Lord protect his disciples so that they remain faithful to God (Jn 17:11). He prays that Simon Peter's "faith may not fail" (Lk 22:32). Thanks to that prayer, Peter, whose faith was wavering, becomes a pillar of strength in the early Church.

Faithfulness rewarded

In the parable of the talents, the master rewards the faithful servant: "Well done, good and faithful servant! You have been faithful with a few things; I will put you in charge of many things. Come and share your master's happiness!" (Mt 25:21).

Impact of our faith on those around us

"I thank my God through Jesus Christ for all of you, because your faith is being reported all over the world" (Ro 1:8). Paul thanks God for the faith of the Christians in the Roman Church. We must never underestimate the impact our own faith can have on those around us.

My faith has often been "boosted" in prayer meetings, listening to brothers and sisters relying on God's promises in prayer. I still have wonderful memories from the prayer meetings in Operation Mobilisation in Catford, near London. George Verwer, the founder of that organisation, prayed with faith that God would give them a ship and the navigation personnel required: captain, officers, sailors, missionaries… to be able to evangelise the world![31]

George, in the middle of the prayer meeting would often start singing spontaneously "Faith is the victory, faith is the victory, oh glorious victory that overcomes the world!" Thanks to George's prayer of faith and the faith of thousands of others around the world. God provided four ships: Logos, Logos II, Doulos and Logos Hope. Through the effective ministry of these ships every year over one million people are reached with the Gospel. Since the beginning of the work of Operation Mobilisation, God has raised up a hundred and fifty thousand young people for the evangelisation of the world.

I also think back to the meetings with Brother Andrew[32] or other members of the Open Doors team who prayed with faith and fervour for God to open the borders of countries closed to the Gospel. These prayers of faith were a real challenge to me as a young Christian and they really encouraged me.

Space for reflection: questions and practical application

1. Why not stop reading now and pray the disciples' short, simple and profound prayer: "Increase my faith, Lord".
2. A verse to memorise: "Let love and faithfulness never leave you; bind them around your neck, write them on the tablet of your heart. Then you will win favour and a good name in the sight of God and man" (Pr 3:3-4).
3. In what areas do you need to practice faithfulness and loyalty: in your relationships, in keeping your word, in your commitments in the Church…?

4. What causes unfaithfulness?

5. Do you know a faithful person at Church? What do they bring or contribute to the Church?

MY PRAYER

Lord, create in me a renewed confidence in the promises of your Word. Help me to rely not on my own thoughts or feelings but on what you tell me in the Bible. I want to be faithful to you in good and bad times. Rescue and deliver me when I am tempted. Help me to be a faithful Christian in the little things. In Jesus' name. Amen.

YOUR PRAYER

____

____

____

____

____

— Gentleness —

> "But the fruit of the Spirit is love, joy, peace, patience, kindness, goodness, faithfulness, **gentleness** and self-control" (Galatians 5:22)

Definition: Gentleness consists of a gesture made with grace, courtesy, kindness, restraint and intelligence. It is accompanied by a "magical charm" which produces extraordinary results.

Isabelle Olekhnovitch gives us a good introduction to this word:

> The *Bible du Semeur* sometimes chooses to translate the word "gentle" with the word "humble" or "kind", perhaps more easily understood by man nowadays. But should gentleness not be rehabilitated? And should we not, finally, move away from macho stereotypes? No, men who show gentleness are not effeminate! No, women who show gentleness are not silly! Gentle is not a synonym for weak, insipid or unpleasantly sweet, it means the opposite of hard, inflexible, intransigent, arrogant, aggressive; it is the synonym of merciful, good, generous.[33]

An African proverb says: "A gentle hand can guide an elephant anywhere".

"Gentle words fall like snowflakes but they carry a lot of weight" (author unknown).

"Primitive man saw gentleness as a contemptible sign of weakness. Aristotle defined it as the balancing point between two extremes: chronic anger and a weak character incapable of indignation. For Plato, gentleness was a natural disposition

> *"Gentle words fall like snowflakes but they carry a lot of weight" (author unknown).*

regulating relationships between men, and the opposite of ferocity or cruelty."[34]

The word "gentleness" has several meanings in the Bible. William Barclay, a Scottish theologian, says in his book[35] that there are three meanings for this word in the New Testament: firstly being capable of **submitting to God's will**: "Blessed are the meek, [also translated as gentle] for they will inherit the earth" (Matt 5:5). In the New Testament, gentleness is far from being a sign of weakness, on the contrary, it is an inner strength which is linked to self-control and is inspired by humility (Eph 4:2).

The second meaning attached to this word is **the ability to welcome and accept God's Word**: "humbly accept the word planted in you, which can save you" (Jas 1:21). The use of the word "humbly" evokes the gentle nature in which the Word should be accepted and that the person should also not be too proud to learn.

The third meaning is **to be attentive and considerate** in our relationships with others. Paul describes "gentleness" very well in his letter to the Ephesians: "Be completely humble and gentle; be patient, bearing with one another in love. Make every effort to keep the unity of the Spirit through the bond of peace" (Eph 4:2-3).

Jesus – our role model for gentleness

"Take my yoke upon you and learn from me, for I am gentle and humble in heart, and you will find rest for your souls" (Mt 11:29).

The prophecy of Zechariah (Zec 9.9) announces Jesus' entrance into Jerusalem, on Palm Sunday: "See, your king comes to you, gentle and riding on a donkey" (Mt 21:5).

Paul responds to his accusers in this way: "By the humility and gentleness of Christ, I appeal to you" (2Co 10:1).

Gentleness: of great value in God's eyes

"…it should be that of your inner self, the unfading beauty of a gentle and quiet spirit, which is of great worth in God's sight" (1Pe 3:4).

Why do we need this gentleness?

To combat sin

To combat sin: "Therefore, get rid of all moral filth and the evil that is so prevalent and humbly accept the word planted in you, which can save you" (Jas 1:21).

To receive the Word in us

This same verse, James 1:21, invites us to receive the Word of God with gentleness, to submit ourselves to it and allow ourselves to be transformed by it. It is in this way that it can convince, instruct and correct us (2Ti 3:16).

To convince and win over our adversaries

There is a Bulgarian proverb which says: "A gentle word can open an iron door".

> *"… it should be that of your inner self, the unfading beauty of a gentle and quiet spirit, which is of great worth in God's sight" (1Pe 3:4).*

Paul explains to the young Timothy that gentleness is indispensable in heated discussions: "And the Lord's servant must not be quarrelsome but must be kind to everyone, able to teach, not resentful. Opponents must be gently instructed, in the hope that God will grant them repentance leading them to a knowledge of the truth" (2Ti 2:24-25).

Here is the J.B. Phillips translation of the text:

> "And the Lord's servant must not be a man of strife: he must be kind to all, ready and able to teach: he must have

> patience and the ability gently to correct t'ose who oppose his message. He must always bear in mind the possibility that God will give them a different outlook, and that they may come to know the truth. They may come to their senses and be rescued from the power of the devil by the servant of the Lord and set to work for God's purposes" (2Ti 2:24-25).

To keep unity

"Be completely humble and gentle; be patient, bearing with one another in love. Make every effort to keep the unity of the Spirit through the bond of peace" (Eph 4:2-3).

Notice that this unity is not automatic. Everyone has to make an effort to create unity through gentleness, and this is possible thanks to the power of the Holy Spirit in our lives. In Church life, it is necessary to know that people are more important than activities. Good relationships in the Church are more important than projects. This fruit of the Spirit, gentleness, will allow us to improve our relationships with others and contribute to the unity of Christ's body.

> *In Church life, it is necessary to know that people are more important than activities.*

To shine

> "Gentleness is a strong quality. We mistake it too easily for spinelessness. The word is used of a horse which has been broken in. It describes the need for our characters to be sensitive to the control of God's touch on the reins so that all the drive, energy and zeal we have can be channelled to good effect. Without that control our zeal can be as useless and destructive as an untamed horse. We may bolt all over the place, knocking over fences and knocking down people, but we shall be of no use to our Master."[36]

The apostle Paul advises Titus to teach: "to slander no one, to be peaceable and considerate, and always to be gentle toward everyone" (Tit 3:2).

When our daughter-in-law came to visit us for the first time, I was out. She arrived at the house before me and was able to have a chat with our neighbours. When I arrived, my neighbour was full of praise for her: "You'll see your future daughter-in-law is considerate, gentle, lovely!" What a testimony! I can confirm today that my neighbour was right.

"Let your gentleness be evident to all. The Lord is near" (Php 4:5).

Space for reflection: questions and practical application

1. Gentleness, is it a typically feminine quality?

2. In which area do you need to practise being gentle: your words, your thoughts about others?

3. If in the last year ten pounds had been put into your bank account for every gentle word or gesture you had made, how much would you have in your account today?

4. If in the last year ten pounds had been removed for every harsh word you had spoken, how much would you have in your account today?

MY PRAYER

My God, grant me humility to consider others more important than me. May my gestures, words and attitudes today be filled with grace, sensitivity and gentleness. I ask all of this in the name of Jesus. Amen.

YOUR PRAYER

____

____

____

____

____

— Self-Control —

"But the fruit of the Spirit is love, joy, peace, patience, kindness, goodness, faithfulness, gentleness and **self-control**" (Galatians 5:22)

The Oxford English dictionary defines self-control as **to be in control of oneself and one's desires**.

Another expression used to convey self-control is self-mastery. The title of Master's degree derives from this word "mastery". To have a Master's degree requires the acquisition of a wide knowledge of the principles and rules of a specific subject. As the Master of a given subject, you have "mastered" the subject and have the necessary knowledge and authority to speak about it.

Self-control is our ability to control our impulses, reactions, feelings and desires.

With the word control, there is also the idea of acquiring a force or power which can be used to combat destructive or damaging elements: for example, fire fighters can **control** a blaze. However, our subject is **self-control** and not the control of a person, subject or element. It is the ability to control our impulses, reactions, feelings and desires. What a prospect! "He that would govern others should first be master of himself" (Philip Massinger).[37]

"He who reigns within himself and rules his passions, desires and fears is more than a king" (John Milton).[38]

To emphasize the importance of this subject, I would first like to explore an idea which is incompatible with self-control: laziness and carelessness. We are given a good example in Proverbs 24:30-34:

> I went past the field of a sluggard, past the vineyard of someone who has no sense; thorns had come up everywhere, the ground was covered with weeds, and the stone wall was in ruins. I applied my heart to what I observed and learned a lesson from what I saw: A little sleep, a little slumber, a little folding of the hands to rest—and poverty will come on you like a thief and scarcity like an armed man.

The scene here is dreadful. It is about a field which has been neglected by a lazy farmer. This man's lethargy is ruining his field (thorns, brambles, crumbling walls…) and leading him into poverty. Notice that poverty is personified (thief, armed man). This field could be our hearts. Are there thorns of bitterness, malice, resentment in our hearts? Brambles of indifference or unbelief?

This is a solemn warning against idleness, carelessness and not being vigilant. Be careful! The devil takes advantage of our laziness to make us numb and drowsy. This lack of vigilance can be in relation to our thoughts, words or acts and could lead to disorder in our lives. Carelessness can be a trap. The enemy surrounds us, he "prowls around like a roaring lion looking for someone to devour" (1Pe 5:8).

Non-vigilance: I missed my flight

Some months ago I was travelling from Glasgow to Montpellier via Paris. I stayed overnight in Paris and had some free time the next day to relax. My Paris – Montpellier flight was at 5pm and the gate closed at 4pm.

I put my feet up, relaxed, read, watched TV, had an afternoon nap…

The day rolled on (and so did the clock). At 3pm I left the hotel and boarded the first bus that came. I soon discovered that I was on the wrong bus going in the wrong direction. It was now 3.30pm. I started to panic and tried to hitch a lift trailing my three suitcases behind me. Fortunately, the airport bus arrived. The end of the story is that I had to run like an athlete to Gate 21 but alas… three minutes too late! I missed my flight to Montpellier.

Only three minutes late? No, I had wasted eight hours, dreaming, dwindling away my time, being lazy and not paying attention to my flight schedule!

Lazy and non-vigilant, just like the man in Proverbs 24.

Another definition: self-control is **the ability to restrain yourself, to overcome, resist and conquer**.

We find our first beautiful image in Proverbs 16:32: "Better a patient person than a warrior, one with self-control than one who takes a city."

Paul refers to self-control and self-discipline when he speaks of the rigorous training an athlete imposes on himself (1Co 9:25) or control in the sexual life of a Christian (1Co 7:9).

"Secular Greek uses it [self-control] of the virtue of an emperor who never lets his private interests influence the government of his people."[39] History shows us that this reference to "self-control" has not always been put into practice.

> *"Better a patient person than a warrior, one with self-control than one who takes a city."*
> *(Pr 16.32)*

In the Old Testament, the expression "self-control" only appears once in Proverbs 25:28: "Like a city whose walls are broken through is a person who lacks self-control."

A lack of self-control: the problems

A person who is not in control of himself is vulnerable and will always be subject to attack and defeat. Samson is a sad example of the consequences of letting oneself go. He let himself doze off in the arms of the beautiful Delilah, who used this to gain access to his heart and to the secret of his strength. Everyone knows how this story continues and ends: Delilah cuts his hair (the source of his strength) and he finishes his life blinded and in chains (Jdg 16), dying under the ruins of the Philistine temple, killing his enemies at the same time as himself.

> *A person who is not in control of himself is vulnerable and will always be subject to attack and defeat.*

Someone who cannot control their anger is violent towards others around him. Someone who consumes too much alcohol loses their composure and becomes a danger to those around them. A lack of self-control creates problems and leads to dangerous situations and disorder.

On our way to our honeymoon in Austria, my wife and I stopped at a small restaurant. We were the only customers. As we were sitting out on the terrace and waiting to order, we overheard the couple who owned the restaurant arguing with one another in the back room. A few minutes later, plates were flying across the room, then chairs and tables… We quickly left the restaurant, wondering if that was what marriage was really like!?

The restaurant owners could not even control themselves in front of the customers. The consequences could be devastating for them. No more customers would mean no more restaurant and they would lose their livelihood as a couple…

Self-control: life

Here is a positive example of self-control: David is being pursued by Saul who is trying to kill him. A unique opportunity presents itself for David to kill Saul easily, to get his revenge once and for all. But David says no to hatred and vengeance, he controls himself and lets his persecutor live: "Who can lay a hand on the LORD's anointed and be guiltless?" (1Sa 26:9).

In the New Testament, self-control can be translated as "temperate" in relation to drinking, but also in a wider sense (1Ti 3:2-3, 11; Tit 2:2).

In human philosophical thought, self-control is the fruit of a power which man has over himself. This is what the Greek philosophers Aristotle, Plato and the Stoics taught: our own ability to master ourselves. This is also what ascetic religions propose, such as Buddhism, which hopes to control the body and the spirit by imposing suffering and hardship on them. These currents of thought go against what is taught in the Bible. Legalism also falls into this trap: you must do this, you must not do that etc.

Notice that self-control is a necessary quality to be a bishop or elder in a Church: "An elder must be [...] hospitable, one who loves what is good, who is self-controlled, upright, holy and disciplined" (Tit 1:6-8).

I learnt a lot from the Swiss love of order. Being organised is a great quality. Someone once said: "When there is order, God's hand is at work".

When there is conflict or disorder in our Churches, it often arises from the private lives of Christians, brothers and sisters who are not able to control or discipline themselves... I am also speaking for myself here.

If I want there to be order in the Church, there must first be order in my private life, in my marriage and family. Everything starts there.

"An elder must be [...] hospitable, one who loves what is good, who is self-controlled, upright, holy and disciplined" (Tit 1:6-8).

As a pastor, I have sometimes wanted to say exactly what I think to someone. However, my wife has calmly prevented me from doing so by saying: "No! You are just going to create problems if you say something. Better to keep it to yourself and pray!" What wisdom and restraint! It is the power of the Holy Spirit, working in me, which produces self-control.

We are not talking here of iron discipline, but rather the positive and constructive discipline of the Holy Spirit which renews us inwardly and gives us an inner peace.

The Holy Spirit: our authority

There was chaos every Friday morning in the Pierrelatte market where I had a Christian bookstall: it was "the law of the jungle", and the first person to arrive got the best place to set up their stall. Having had a stall there for a long time, I had a fixed spot and I was not worried that someone would take it. However, as the weeks progressed, I noticed that my spot was getting smaller.

> *We are not talking here of iron discipline, but rather the positive and constructive discipline of the Holy Spirit which renews us inwardly and gives us an inner peace.*

One day, when I was no longer able to put up my four metre stall, I asked my neighbours to move theirs back slightly. But everyone blamed someone else. What could I do? I had two solutions: I could either roll up my sleeves and fight with them in the middle of the market (which would not have been a very good testimony) or I could seek out the local policeman, the man with authority who knew the lay-out and exact space allotted to every person selling merchandise. I went to find him and asked him to put everything in order; which he did without any difficulty! I thereafter had three metres extra!

Someone with authority knew how to deal with and control the situation and that is very important! This also helps us to understand the meaning of the word "self-control": **with the help of the Holy Spirit**, we can put limits on things which should not be in our lives, which impede us and even make us and others stumble.

This ability to control oneself and allow the Spirit of God to act in our private lives, bringing peace into our hearts, will have an impact on all of our relationships. If we do not have that peace in us, we will be at war with others and with God. This inner peace will allow us to enrich and strengthen our relationships in our families, Church and society.

This ability to control oneself and allow the Spirit of God to act in our private lives, bringing peace into our hearts, will have an impact on all of our relationships.

Self-control: a collaboration between God and me

> "His divine power has given us everything we need for a godly life through our knowledge of him who called us by his own glory and goodness. Through these he has given us his very great and precious promises, so that through them you may participate in the divine nature, **having escaped the corruption in the world caused by evil desires**.
> For this very reason, make every effort to add to your faith goodness; and to goodness, knowledge; and to knowledge, **self-control**; and to self-control, perseverance; and to perseverance, godliness; and to godliness, mutual affection; and to mutual affection, love" (2Pe 1:3-7).

This text gives us two key principles to enable us to bear fruit: love, perseverance (patience), self-control (v.6-7).

The first key is to **understand and appreciate what God has already given us**:

- His divine power, his Holy Spirit within us (v.3).
- His calling (v.3).
- Precious promises (v.4).

The second key is to **understand our responsibility and add** to our knowledge, self-control, patience, godliness (all the qualities which grow and strengthen our relationship with God), mutual affection and love.

The verb "add" is very interesting in Greek. It "refers back to the "chorege", a rich Greek citizen who voluntarily financed choirs to enrich and embellish theatrical productions".[40] God is the director and producer and we are his "choreges". We have our part to play. It is up to us to do all that we can to cultivate the fruit of the Spirit.

In this collaboration, there is a promise: "For if you possess these qualities in increasing measure, they will keep you from being ineffective and unproductive in your knowledge of our Lord Jesus Christ" (v.8).

What a contrast to the farmer in Proverbs 24 who is lazy and lets himself go!

Let us look at some areas in our life where we may need self-control

Our tongues

"We all stumble in many ways. Anyone who is never at fault in what they say is perfect, able to keep their whole body in check" (Jas 3:2).

Anger

"Whoever is patient has great understanding, but one who is quick-tempered displays folly" (Pr 14:29).

Eating or drinking excessively

"Since an overseer manages God's household, he must be blameless—not overbearing, not quick-tempered, **not given to drunkenness**, not violent, not pursuing dishonest gain. Rather, he must be hospitable, one who loves what is good, who is self-controlled, upright, holy and disciplined. He must hold firmly to the trustworthy message as it has been taught, so that he can encourage others by sound doctrine and refute those who oppose it" (Tit 1:7-9).

"Sow a thought, and you reap an act; Sow an act, and you reap a habit; Sow a habit and you reap a character; Sow a character, and you reap a destiny" (author unknown).

Our thoughts

This is an area in my private life in which I need to exercise more self-control.

The following phrase has been attributed to many different people: "Sow a thought, and you reap an act; Sow an act, and you reap a habit; Sow a habit and you reap a character; Sow a character, and you reap a destiny."

We are called to love God with all our mind (thoughts) in Luke 10:27.

Hatred, adultery, jealousy, bitterness… all of these fruits of the flesh originate in our thoughts.

"The LORD saw how great the wickedness of the human race had become on the earth, and that **every inclination of the thoughts** of the human heart was only evil all the time" (Ge 6:5).

"Knowing their thoughts, Jesus said, "Why do you entertain **evil thoughts** in your hearts?" (Mt 9:4).

It is therefore important to win the battle over our thoughts. But how do we go about it?

Martin Luther said: ""You cannot keep birds from flying over your head but you can keep them from building a nest in your hair."[41]

Some practical advice

Enrich your thoughts with God's Word

In John 15:7-8, Jesus says: "If you remain in me and my words remain in you, ask whatever you wish, and it will be done for you. This is to my Father's glory, that you bear much fruit, showing yourselves to be my disciples."

I would like to encourage you to take a verse from the Bible with you each day or week and fill your mind with it. Jesus said if "my words remain in you"; he is not just talking about understanding what we read intellectually and learning it by heart, but allowing the Word to take root in us and transform us. God's living Word will have an impact on our thoughts.

Filter your thoughts

Around 60,000 thoughts go through our minds each day! That makes 1,800,000 a month! It is therefore difficult to control them all. But we can start by sorting them out by using the filter suggested in Philippians 4:8: "Finally, brothers and sisters, whatever is true, whatever is noble, whatever is right, whatever is pure, whatever is lovely, whatever is admirable—if anything is excellent or praiseworthy—think about such things."

Imprison some thoughts

"We demolish arguments and every pretension that sets itself up against the knowledge of God, and we **take captive every thought** to make it obedient to Christ" (2Co 10:5).

We have to "imprison" our evil thoughts. How? By invoking the name of Jesus and calling on his authority. Because there is power in his name. That is why Jesus asks us to preach, baptise and chase out demons in his name.

At my school in Scotland there were lots of trouble makers. I was terrified of them all and did everything I could to avoid them.

Yet, when a fight broke out in the playground, I took a malicious pleasure in watching and would make comments to egg on my friends who were in the "ring".

One day, as I was leaving school on my own, I found myself surrounded by twelve big guys who said: "you, the little smart Alcc who was making comments yesterday, it's your turn to enter the ring!" I was trembling from head to foot but managed to control myself. I suddenly had the great idea of mentioning my class mate Jimmy, (who was built like a wardrobe, and had a reputation as a tough guy): "Perhaps you know my class-mate Jimmy..." I had hardly pronounced his name when the entire group scarpered like terrified rabbits! And I stood there, alone, completely bewildered!

Jesus' name carries with it all of his work, and behind his work, authority and power.

Jimmy's name came with a reputation, authority and power!

Jesus' name carries with it all of his work, and behind his work, authority and power. When evil thoughts invade our minds, we can drive them out in Jesus' name.

Abandon evil thoughts

"Repent, then, and turn to God, so that your sins may be wiped out, that times of refreshing may come from the Lord, and that he may send the Messiah, who has been appointed for you–even Jesus" (Ac 3:19-20). Do you know this liberating power, which breaks the devil's hold on our lives: repentance?

Give new direction to your thoughts

"Yet this I call to mind and therefore I have hope: Because of the Lord's great love we are not consumed, for his compassions never fail. They are new every morning; great is your faithfulness. I say to myself, "The Lord is my portion; therefore I will wait for him"

(La 3:21-24). We can give our thoughts new direction by reading God's Word.

"Do not conform to the pattern of this world, but be transformed by the renewing of your mind. Then you will be able to test and approve what God's will is—his good, pleasing and perfect will" (Ro 12:2). God wants to renew our minds and transform our thoughts. The word "transform" is the same as "transfigure" as it is used in the transfiguration of Jesus in Matthew 17:2. It is also the same as metamorphosis, which means a radical internal change. Our thoughts are often influenced by external sources, the media, what people say etc. So how does this inner renewal work? Through the influence of God's Word on our thoughts. Jesus prays in John 17:17: "Sanctify them by the truth; your word is truth". Speaking of the Church, Paul says in Ephesians 5:26: "to make her holy, cleansing her by the washing with water through the word"; this Word is useful for teaching, convincing and **correcting** (2Ti 3:16). This is why we are invited to meditate on the Word day and night (Jos 1:8), to study it (Ac 17:11), to place it in our hearts (Dt 6:6). This makes me think of the following lesson:

"If you place a cup filled with coffee (or another liquid) under a running tap, the coffee gradually disappears from the cup to be replaced by water. Let's fill our thoughts with the Word of God!

Whenever I spend time filling my mind with God's attributes, his capabilities and kindnesses, there is no longer any room in my head for worries and troubles.

Sow good thoughts

Through prayer. Pray for one another, as the apostle Paul did for the Colossians (Col 1:9-11). Not just "Lord, bless my brother", it will be a profound prayer that they may be filled with the knowledge of God's will, for wisdom and spiritual understanding in order to live a life worthy of the Lord and bear fruit. What a rich and profound prayer! Let's sow good thoughts and create strong bonds between us through prayer.

There are certainly other areas which I could have spoken of, such as our management of money, our sex lives etc. It is important to show moderation in all things.

> *"Search me, God, and know my heart; test me and know my anxious thoughts. See if there is any offensive way in me, and lead me in the way everlasting" (Ps 139:23-24).*

Paul is unequivocal when he says: "'I have the right to do anything,' you say—but not everything is beneficial. 'I have the right to do anything'—but I will not be mastered by anything" (1Co 6:12).

The Holy Spirit, through the Word of God, invites us to examine and sound out our lives. It is easy for me to look at others and criticise them. On the other hand, I really struggle to look at my own faults and examine my own heart. But this is what God wants me to do.

"Search me, God, and know my heart test me and know my anxious thoughts. See if there is any offensive way in me, and lead me in the way everlasting" (Ps 139:23-24).

E. Stanley Jones said: "The Bible redirects my will, cleanses my emotions, enlightens my mind, and quickens my total being."[42]

Space for reflection: questions and practical application

With the help of the table below, I invite you to stand before God and examine your life in specific areas.

1. Put the areas you need to work on in order of priority. For example, for me it would be:

   1.Thoughts, 2. Patience, 3. Anger

2. What to do? – In this column, write down what action you need to take. For example: dedicate an hour a week to reading a good Christian book.
3. When? – Example: choose a date.
4. With whom? – I can choose a close friend, a "coach" who will come alongside me, advise me, encourage me and pray for me.

1. Area	*2. What to do?*	*3. When?*	*4. With whom ? (coach)*
Words			
Thoughts	Enrich my thoughts reading good books for an hour a week	From…	
Anger			
Drink/Food			
Reading			

Films			
Social life			
Body Sex life			
Internet			
Prayer life			
Sleep			
Other...			

A promise to hold onto

"Now to him who is able to do immeasurably more than all we ask or imagine, according to his power that is at work within us, to him be glory in the Church and in Christ Jesus throughout all generations, for ever and ever! Amen" (Eph 3:20-21).

MY PRAYER

Lord, you see the bad habit which is poisoning my life. I cannot get rid of it on my own. I want now to renounce this sin of ________ just now and nail it to the cross. By the power of your Holy Spirit, deliver me from this sin! Rule over me. In Jesus' powerful name. Amen.

YOUR PRAYER

____

____

____

____

____

____

____

— How do you cultivate the fruit of the Spirit? —

Never forget that the sinful nature and the Spirit are at war

The fruit of the Spirit and the works of the flesh (sinful nature) are in constant conflict. Matthew 7:17 and Galatians 5:16-21 both speak of "bad fruits" and those which are "contrary to the fruit of the Spirit": *the works of the flesh.*

Galatians 5:16-21 gives us a list of these works of the flesh:

> "So I say, walk by the Spirit, and you will not gratify the desires of the flesh. For the flesh desires what is contrary to the Spirit, and the Spirit what is contrary to the flesh. They are in conflict with each other, so that you are not able to do what you want. But if you are led by the Spirit, you are not under the law.
> The acts of the flesh are obvious: sexual immorality, impurity and debauchery; idolatry and witchcraft; hatred, discord, jealousy, fits of rage, selfish ambition, dissensions, factions and envy; drunkenness, orgies, and the like. I warn you, as I did before, that those who live like this will not inherit the kingdom of God."

> *The fruit of the Spirit and the works of the flesh are in constant conflict.*

The works of the flesh can be put into four different categories or themes. In the first group are sins related to sexual relations: sexual immorality, impurity and debauchery. In the second group are those sins relating to occultism: idolatry and magic. The third group concerns relationships: hatred, discord, jealousy, fits of rage, selfish ambition, dissentions, factions and envy. The fourth and last group has extreme appetites as its theme: drunkenness, orgies etc.

Fruits of the Flesh (Gal 5:17-21)	Fruit of the Spirit (Gal 5:22)
Sex : sexual immorality impurity debauchery	Relationship with God: love joy peace
OPPOSITION	
Occultism: idolatry magic	Relationship with others: patience kindness goodness
Relationships: hatred - discord jealousy - fits of rage selfish ambition - envy dissentions - factions	Relationship with ourselves: faithfulness gentleness self-control
Appetites: drunkenness - orgies	
WAR	

We previously noted how the fruit of the Spirit will have a positive impact on our relationships at all levels: with God, with others and with ourselves. The works of the flesh will also have an impact, but this time negative, on our relationships: **with God** – idolatry and all the other sins separate us from him; **with others** – hatred, discord, jealousy, fits of rage, selfish ambition, envy, dissentions and factions create tensions which often lead to the breakdown of relationships; **with ourselves** – drunkenness, impurity and depravity lead to low self-esteem and guilt.

War has been declared between the sinful nature and the Spirit

It is an invisible, spiritual war which takes place in "the heavenly realms" (Eph 6:12). Satan is at the root of all the works of the flesh. Some preachers want to make us believe that the Christian life is a walk in the park. "Come to Jesus and all your problems will be solved!" No! Nothing could be further from the truth! The Bible never tells us this! On the contrary, Jesus tells us: "In this world you will have trouble" (Jn 16:33). Paul says the same thing to the Thessalonians: "we kept telling you that we would be persecuted" (1Th 3:4). The devil's goal is to hinder God's work. If he can affect the Christian he will have achieved his purpose.

Paul was not ignorant of Satan's intentions or schemes: "For we are not unaware of his schemes" (2Co 2:11).

> *It's an invisible, spiritual war which takes place in "the heavenly realms" (Eph 6:12).*

What does the devil do?

- He prowls around us like a lion (1Pe 5:8).
- He blinds us to the message of the Gospel (2Co 4:4).
- He attempts to remove God's Word from people's hearts as soon as it is sown (Mt 13:19).
- He sows doubt: "Did God really say…" (Ge 3:1).
- He accuses the just (Zec 3:1).
- He attacks and afflicts the man of God (Job 1:12).
- He tempts (Mt 4:1).
- He wants to ruin the soul and the body (Lk 9:42).
- He is a liar (Jn 8:44).
- He disguises himself as "an angel of light" (2Co 11:14).
- He encourages sin (Jn 13:2).

- He sows disorder (Mt 13:38).
- He twists the Scriptures (Mt 4:6).

What we can do: declare war on him!

How do we do this?

Be equipped with the armour and weapons of God

In Ephesians 6:11-17, Paul tells us to "Put on the full armour of God, so that you can take your stand against the devil's schemes". This armour and these weapons, forged and provided by God himself, will help us to resist the devil, "stand firm" and be on the offensive.

The enemy is well organised and has many "agents":

"For our fight is not against any physical enemy: it is against organisations and powers that are spiritual. We are up against the unseen power that controls this dark world, and spiritual agents from the very headquarters of evil" (v.12, J.B. Phillips).

During a conference, the great English theologian John Stott said that every day, after washing and dressing, he launched into his day by praying and putting on the armour of God piece by piece: the belt of truth, the breastplate of righteousness, the sandals to carry the Gospel to others, the shield of faith, the helmet of salvation and the sword of the Spirit.

Recognise that this invisible, internal battle exists

In Romans 7:19, the apostle Paul said: "For I do not do the good I want to do, but the evil I do not want to do". Why? Because there is a tug-of-war taking place within him, two powers are confronting one another. It is like two dogs fighting. Which one will win, would you say? It all depends on which one you feed! Are we allowing the Holy Spirit to work in us, do we give him all the space he needs to develop the fruit of the Spirit in us – not leaving any room for the works of the flesh and Satan?

Resist the devil

Be careful not to play with fire and let the devil send your will to sleep.

Be careful not to play with fire and let the devil send your will to sleep! You have to resist him: "Resist the devil, and he will flee from you" (Jas 4:7). How? Jesus resisted the devil by quoting the Word of God (Mt 4:1-11). He used the Word of God as a sword: "For the word of God is alive and active. Sharper than any double-edged sword" (Heb 4:12).

Be strong in the Lord

In this battle against the sinful nature, it is important to be strong so that on a "bad day" you can stand firm. The bad day could be, for example, when I'm tired, irritated, feeling lazy… the day I forget to be vigilant. It is at that moment that I will give in to the temptation to criticise a brother or sister, to get carried away, to look at images or films on the internet which tarnish me and sadden the Holy Spirit.

"Be strong—not in yourselves but in the Lord, in the power of his boundless resource. (Eph 6:10, J.B. Phillips)

Choose whom to serve: the flesh or the Spirit?

You have to make a decision where to position yourself and not change sides. We cannot have a foot in more than one camp.

Jesus tells us, in Matthew 6:24, when speaking about money and love: "No one can serve two masters. Either you will hate the one and love the other, or you will be devoted to the one and despise the other. You cannot serve both God and money."

"Be strong—not in yourselves but in the Lord, in the power of his boundless resource. (Eph 6:10, J.B. Phillips)

Joshua tells the Israelites what they must do: "choose for yourselves this day whom you will serve." He had already chosen his camp: "But as for me and my household, we will serve the LORD" (Jos 24:15).

My grandfather on my mother's side was a huge fan of football. He had signed up his eldest son John in a local club. Each time that John came back from a match, he talked about his team's exploits and, most importantly, the part he had played in their victory. One day, my grandfather discreetly took a seat in the stadium to watch his son play a match. That evening, at dinner, my grandfather asked John if he had played well in his match that day. John bragged about the goal he had scored. "You're right, his Dad replied, you scored a goal... but it was against your own team!" In the same way, we can tell people that we are Christians and are led by the Spirit but, at the same time, we can allow the sinful nature to dominate our words and actions. This scores us goals against our own team, gives points to the devil and saddens the Holy Spirit.

Every day, we make decisions which will have repercussions, which will bear good or bad fruit: what we choose to read, how we use our free time, abilities and gifts, how we invest our money, our words etc. Last weekend, I was visiting another Church and I met a man who I will call "Peter". He was not a leader in the Church, just a member.

Peter had chosen his camp. At the end of the service, he was the one to get the hoover out and start cleaning. He also gave lifts to and from the Church to his friends who didn't have cars. It was Peter who, for a whole year, took lessons in Arabic so he could communicate better with the Syrian refugees who had recently arrived in his town. He also gave free guitar lessons to friends at Church. He was the one who hosted Bible study groups before the Church was planted. He was also the one who prepared my picnic and drove me to the station. Peter had chosen to let himself be led by the Holy Spirit?

Whom do you want to serve, the flesh? Or the Spirit?

"Crucify" the sinful nature

"Those who belong to Christ Jesus have crucified the flesh with its passions and desires" (Gal 5:24).

John Stott also reminds us: "When some jealous, or proud, or malicious, or impure thought invades our mind, we must kick it out at once. It is fatal to begin to examine it and consider whether we are going to give in to it or not. We have declared war on it; we are not going to resume negotiations. We have settled the issue for good; we are not going to re-open it. We have crucified the flesh; we are never going to draw out the nails."[43]

I was once told of someone who would pray each time they were tempted: "Lord, deliver me from this sin, but not straight away". Our sins have been nailed to the cross and we have to let them die there!

Crucifixion was a slow and painful death. Crucifying the works of the flesh does involve suffering. It is an act which needs to be carried out whenever necessary. The disciple of Jesus will "take up their cross daily" (Lk 9.23). Do you want to experience that liberating power which only Jesus can bestow? Is your life currently poisoned by a bad habit or sin which saddens you? Do you want to be set free? Stop reading here and take a moment to say to Jesus that you want to nail that sin to the cross right now!

Because we belong to Christ and because of what he did for us on the cross, we have been called to voluntarily give up the passions and desires of the flesh: "Those who belong to Christ have crucified their old nature with all that it loved and lusted for. If our lives are centred in the Spirit, let us be guided by the Spirit" (Gal 5:25, J.B. Phillips).

Letting yourself be led by the Spirit and walking in accordance with the Spirit

These are two very different actions: the first is passive and the second is active. It is the Spirit who leads and we walk alongside him.

I really like the image of the sailing boat which uses the wind in its sails to make headway or change direction. **Letting yourself be**

led by the Spirit, means being sensitive to his presence and power in every area of your life and allowing him to influence and change your character. "Jesus, full of the Holy Spirit, left the Jordan and was led by the Spirit into the wilderness" (Lk 4:1). It means "carried along by the Holy Spirit" (2Pe 1:21).

> *Letting yourself be led by the Spirit, means being sensitive to his presence and power in every area of your life and allowing him to influence and change your character.*

We must not forget that the Holy Spirit reveals sin (Jn 16:8), he teaches us and reminds us of God's Word (Jn 14:26). He opens or closes doors: "Paul and his companions travelled throughout the region of Phrygia and Galatia, having been kept by the Holy Spirit from preaching the word in the province of Asia" (Ac 16:6).

By being sensitive to the presence and direction of the Holy Spirit in our day-to-day lives, we are able to **walk** and move forward in our Christian lives.

John Stott explains that the word "walk" in Galatians 5:16 and 25 has two different meanings in Greek: "The English of both verses 16 and 25 contains the verb to "walk", but the Greek words are different. The verb in verse 16 is the ordinary one for walking, but that in verse 25 (*stoicheô*) refers literally to people being "drawn up in line" (…) So to "walk by the Spirit" is deliberately to walk along the path or according to the line which the Holy Spirit lays down."[44]

This makes us think of a soldier who, along with his unit, advances under the command of a superior. He does not drag his feet or just do what he wants. **Walking with the Spirit** involves listening to and obeying our leader: the Spirit. The obedience allows us to remain "in line" with him.

Another image is that of the Olympic athlete who must run in his own track. If he goes over the lines, he will be disqualified.

"Walking with the Spirit" requires vigilance and constant attention. Let's walk in the Spirit's track! Our whole life will be permeated by his influence, as for example:

Our thoughts

"Whatever is true, whatever is noble, whatever is right, whatever is pure, whatever is lovely, whatever is admirable—if anything is excellent or praiseworthy—think about such things" (Php 4:8).

Our plans and ambitions

"Since, then, you have been raised with Christ, set your hearts on things above, where Christ is, seated at the right hand of God. Set your minds on things above, not on earthly things" (Col 3:1-2).

Our relationships

"Since we live by the Spirit, let us keep in step with the Spirit. Let us not become conceited, provoking and envying each other" (Gal 5:25-26).

Remain attached to the vine

Jesus said: "I am the vine; you are the branches. If you remain in me and I in you, you will bear much fruit; apart from me you can do nothing" (Jn 15:5). This constant attachment to Jesus, through prayer and daily contact with his Word, will allow the sap of the vine to reach the shoots which will then bear good fruits.

Remaining attached to the vine means fully trusting in all of God's promises.

Remain attached to "the better promises" (Heb 8:6)

The promises in God's Word are greater than the devil's attractive but deceitful proposals.

> *The promises in God's Word are greater than the devil's attractive but deceitful proposals.*

When we get board a Boeing 747, we are capable of flying. Why is that? Because the aircraft has powerful engines which can overcome the laws of gravity. On our own, we would be incapable of flying that high. In the same way, the greater power of God's promises towers above the law of sin and defeats it. As long as I hold onto these promises, I am victorious over the flesh. As soon as I think I can manage on my own, without the help of the Holy Spirit, I am guaranteed to fall.

Be like Jesus and embody the fruit of the Spirit

We must never forget that God gives us the nine fruits of the Spirit so that we can reflect the character of Christ like a mirror. "For those God foreknew he also **predestined to be conformed to the image of his Son**, that he might be the firstborn among many brothers and sisters" (Ro 8:29). Do you know a joyful, patient, faithful, gentle, kind Christian who is filled with Christ's love? They are incredibly effective evangelists!

Understand the final goal

In John 15:8, Jesus tells us why we are given the fruit of the Spirit: "This is to **my Father's glory**, that you bear much fruit, showing yourselves to be my disciples."

In his book *I Believe in the Holy Spirit*, Michael Green points out that: "The Holy Spirit does not draw attention to himself. He is there to glorify Jesus, to show Jesus' attractiveness and not to take the centre of the stage."[45]

The goal of the fruit of the Spirit is **to glorify God**. In the Old Testament, this glory is demonstrated through creation, God's presence in the tabernacle, then in the temple and through his interventions. In the New Testament, Jesus and the action of the

Holy Spirit show his glory. Theologians tell us that God's glory is the sum-total of everything that God, Father, Son and Holy Spirit, is, does and says.

It is like a vase filled with flowers: there is a flower for each one of God's attributes, a flower for each of Jesus' teachings, a flower for each intervention of the Holy Spirit… This vase of flowers gives off a beautiful scent: the glory of God.

MY PRAYER

My Father, I have often given in to temptation during this spiritual battle. I am sorry and I repent. I have saddened the Holy Spirit and have distanced myself from you and your Word.

"Have mercy on me, O God,
according to your unfailing love;
according to your great compassion
blot out my transgressions.
Wash away all my iniquity
and cleanse me from my sin.

For I know my transgressions,
and my sin is always before me.
Against you, you only, have I sinned [...]

Cleanse me with hyssop, and I will be clean;
wash me, and I will be whiter than snow.
Let me hear joy and gladness;
let the bones you have crushed rejoice.
Hide your face from my sins
and blot out all my iniquity.

Create in me a pure heart, O God,
and renew a steadfast spirit within me" (Ps 51:1-10).

Thank you for your forgiveness. Help me to resist the devil, to put on all the armour of God and flee from temptation. I want to strengthen myself in you, Lord, to crucify the desires of the sinful nature and keep in step with the Holy Spirit.

I ask this in Jesus's powerful name. Amen.

YOUR PRAYER

— Conclusion —
Do you want to be a beautiful fruit tree?

The tree in Psalm 1 has two qualities: it **yields its fruit in season**, meaning it is a useful tree which is regularly in bloom; its **leaves do not wither**: it remains constant, perseveres and is full of vitality. Its secret is that it is planted by streams of water which nourish, refresh and renew it.

To cultivate the fruit of the Spirit, we need to stay close to the source of living water: Jesus and his Word.

I would like to conclude with a beautiful quotation from Michael Green:

> "This powerful, victorious Spirit which indwells believers, and can keep their sinful natures nailed upon the cross, is like a seed planted in the soil of the believer's life. If cultivated and nourished, this seed will grow into a lovely fruitful tree; and this is what the fruit is like: love, joy, peace, patience, kindness, goodness, faithfulness, gentleness, self-control."[46]

I would like to be a beautiful tree which bears lots of good fruit. What about you?

— Practical Decisions —

Having read this work, I would now like to invite you to make some practical, concrete decisions to cultivate each fruit of the Spirit in your life.

Love

___

___

___

Joy

___

___

___

Peace

___

___

___

Patience

___

___

___

___

Kindness

Goodness

Faithfulness

Gentleness

Self-control

— Notes —

Introduction

1. Warren W. Wiersbe, *Galatians. Be free*, Wheaton, Victoria Books, 1975, p 134.
2. Translated from J.-M. Nicole, *Précis de doctrine chrétienne*, Nogent-sur-Marne, Éditions de l'institut, 1986, p. 219-220.

Introduction to Galatians 5:22

3. John Stott, *The message of Galatians*, Leicester, Inter-Varsity Press, 1988, p. 21-22.

Chapter 1. Love

4. Hazel Offner, *Fruit of the Spirit—Nine studies for individuals or groups*, Bletchley, Scripture Union, 2006, p. 9.
5. Quoted by John Blanchard in *The Complete Gathered Gold*, Darlington, Evangelical Press, 2007, p. 388.
6. George Sweeting, *Great Quotes and illustrations - Love*, Milton Keynes, Word Publishing, 1985, p. 177.
7. William Barclay, *The Letters to the Galatians and Ephesians*, Edinburgh, Saint Andrew Press, 2002, p. 60.
8. Quoted by John Blanchard, *The Complete Gathered Gold*, Darlington, Evangelical Press, 2007, p. 389.
9. J.-M Nicole, *Précis de doctrine chrétienne*, Nogent-sur-Marne, Editions de l'Institut Biblique, 7e éd., 2006, p. 60 and note 9; "Scripture underlines the fact that "the Father loves the Son" (John 5.20, etc.) and that "the Son loves the Father" (John 14.31).

10. James Packer, *Knowing God*, London, Hodder & Stoughton, 1993, p. 140.

11. *Ibid.*, p. 133.

12. Translated from J.-M. Nicole, *Précis de doctrine chrétienne*, Nogent-sur-Marne, Editions de l'Institut Biblique, 7e ed., 2006, p. 220.

13. Translated from J.-M. Nicole, *Précis de doctrine chrétienne*, Nogent-sur-Marne, Editions de l'Institut Biblique, 7e ed., 2006, p. 221.

14. Quoted by John Blanchard, *The Complete Gathered Gold*, Darlington, Evangelical Press, 2007, p. 388.

15. Words & Music © 1923, Ren. 1951 by Hope Publishing Co., Carol Stream, IL 60188.

Chapter 2. Joy

16. *Nouveau Dictionnaire Biblique*, Saint-Légier, Editions Emmaüs, 2012, p. 690.

17. Frédéric Lenoir, *La puissance de la joie*, Paris, Fayard, 2015.

18. Quoted by Rosemarie Jarski, *A Word from the Wise*, Random House, Ebury Press, 2006, p. 281.

19. Quoted by John Blanchard, *The Complete Gathered Gold*, Darlington, Evangelical Press, 2007, p. 359.

20. James Packer, *Knowing God, London*, Hodder & Stoughton, 1993, p. 16.

21. See "Others books in English by Ian Newberry" at the end of this book (p. 165).

22. Quoted by Charles R. Swindoll, *Swindoll's Ultimate Book of Illustrations and Quotes*, Nashville, Thomas Nelson Publishers, 1998, p. 323.

23. Quoted by John Blanchard, *The Complete Gathered Gold*, Darlington, Evangelical Press, 2007, p. 357.

Chapter 3. Peace

24. Josh McDowell, *More than a carpenter*, Tyndale House Publishers, 2004.

25. George Appleton, *The Oxford Book of Prayer*, Oxford, Oxford University Press, 1988, p. 75.

Chapter 4. Patience

26. Bob Phillips, *Book of Great Thoughts Funny Sayings*, Carol Stream, Tyndale House Publishers, 1993, p. 240.

27. Roger Steer, *George Müller – delighted in God*, Sevenoaks, Harold Shaw Publishers, 1987, p. 247.

Chapter 5. Kindness and Goodness

28. John Blanchard, *The Complete Gathered Gold*, Darlington, Evangelical Press, 2006, p. 365.

29. John Blanchard, *The Complete Gathered Gold*, Darlington, Evangelical Press, 2006, p. 427.

30. To know more of John Wesley read Hugh Price Hughes, *The Journal of John Wesley*, Chicago, Moody Press Publication.

Chapter 6. Faithfulness

31. To know more of the work and message of Operation Mobilisation, consult George Verwer's books: *No Turning Back*, *Out of the Comfort Zone*, *Drops from a leaking tap…*

32. Brother Andrews' ministry can be found in the following titles : *The Calling*, Open Doors International, Summit Publishing, 1996; *God's Smuggler*, Baker, 2015 (1st ed. 1964); *And God changed his mind*, Chosen Books, 1999.

Chapter 7. Gentleness

33. Translated from Isabelle Olekhnovitch, *Les yeux fixés sur Jésus. 30 jours vers la sainteté*, Charols, Excelsis, 2013, p. 100-101.
34. Translated from *Nouveau Dictionnaire Biblique, révisé et augmenté*, Saint-Légier (Suisse), Éditions Emmaüs, 2012, p. 364.
35. William Barclay, *The letters to the Galatians and Ephesians*, Edinburgh, Saint Andrew Press, 2002, p. 62.
36. Derek J. Tidball, *Skilful Shepherds. Explorations in pastoral theology*, Leicester, IVP, 1997, p. 307.

Chapter 8. Self-control

37. John Cook, *The Book of Positive Quotations*, Minneapolis, Fairview Press, 1997, p. 177.
38. *Ibid.*
39. William Barclay, *The letters to the Galatians and Ephesians*, Edinburgh, St Andrew Press, 2002, p. 62.
40. Translated from *Bible d'étude, version du Semeur*, Charols, Éditions Excelsis, 2000, note on 2 Peter 1.5, p. 1923.
41. Translated from Lettre à Hieronymus Weller (19.6.1530), *WA Br* 5, 374, n° 1593. Quoted in *Martin Luther prédicateur. Arrêts sur images*, Textes choisis et présentés par Albert et Françoise Greiner, Vaux-sur-Seine / Cléon d'Andran, Édifac/ Excelsis, 2002, p. 60.
42. John Blanchard, *The Complete Gathered Gold*, Darlington, Evangelical Press, 2006, p. 50.

Chapter 9. How do you cultivate the fruit of the Spirit?

43. John Stott, *The message of Galatians*, Leicester, Inter-Varsity Press, 1988, p. 152.

44. John Stott, *The Message of Galatians*, Leicester, Inter-Varsity Press, 1988, p. 152-153.

45. Michael Green, *I believe in the Holy Spirit*, London, Hodder and Stoughton, 1978, p. 52.

Conclusion – Do you want to be a beautiful fruit tree?

46. Michael Green, *I believe in the Holy Spirit*, London, Hodder and Stoughton, 1978, p. 88.

— Bibliography to help you go further… —

Barclay William, *The letters to the Galatians and Ephesians*, Saint Andrews Press (Edinburgh, 2002).

Green Michael, *I Believe in the Holy Spirit*, Hodder and Stoughton (London-Sydney-Auckland-Toronto, 1978).

Green Michael, *I believe in Satan's Downfall*, Hodder and Stoughton (London-Sydney-Auckland-Toronto, 1984).

Griffiths Michael, *The Example of Jesus*, Hodder and Stoughton (London-Sydney-Auckland-Toronto, 1985).

Griffiths Michael, *Cinderella with Amnesia*, Inter-Varsity Press (London, 1976).

Griffiths Michael, *Take My Life*, Inter-Varsity Press (Leicester, 1979).

Jones Dr. M.L., *Spiritual Depression, Its Cause and Cure*, Marshall and Pickering (London, 1965).

Maiden Peter, *Building on the Rock*, Monarch Books (Oxford-Grand Rapids, 2016).

Maiden Peter, *Discipleship*, Authentic Media (Keswick, 2007).

Newberry Ian, *Available for God*, Editions Biblos (Pierrelatte, France, 2017).

Offner Hazel, *Fruit of the Spirit, Nine studies for individual groups*, Scripture Union (Bletchly, 2006).

Packer James, *Knowing God*, Hodder and Stoughton (London, 1993).

Packer James, *A Passion for Holiness*, Crossway Books (Nottingham, 1992).

Steer Roger, *George Müller Delighted in God*, Harold Shaw Publishers (Sevenoaks, 1987).

Stott John, *The Cross of Christ*, Inter-Varsity Press (Leicester, 2006)

Stott John, *The Message of Galatians*, Inter-Varsity Press (Leicester, 2006).

Tozer A.W., *The Attributes of God–A Journey into the Father's Heart*, Wing Spread Publishers (Chicago, 2007).

Verwer George, *The Verwer Collection: Revolution of Love – No Turning Back – Hunger for Reality*, Authentic Lifestyle (Bucks, 2006).

Verwer George, *Out of the Comfort Zone*, Authentic Lifestyle (Bucks, 2000).

Verwer George, *Drops from a Leaking Tap*, Authentic Lifestyle (Bucks, 2009).

Warren W. Wiersbe, *Be free, an Expository Study of Galatians*, Victor Books (Wheaton 1980).

— Would you like to organize a seminar? —

If you are interested about the possibility of organizing a seminar on any of the following subjects:

– How to structure and deepen your prayer life: *Back to Basics, back to God.*

– Prayer in the Church: *At the Heart of Prayer.*

– Fasting and prayer in the Bible: *Available for God.*

– How to revive the prayer meeting: *I Believe in Prayer.*

– How to encourage yourself, your family and your Church.

– How to cultivate the fruit of the Spirit: *Cultivating the Fruit of the Spirit.*

– Cultivating your inner garden.

Please write to:

Ian Newberry
c/o Editions Biblos
6 ter Av. Teilhard de Chardin
26700 Pierrelatte
France

Or make contact via our Website: www.enviedeprier.com

— Other books by Ian Newberry —

Back to Basics, Back to God — Personal Prayer

This book gives practical ideas on how to organize and deepen your prayer life: Motivation for prayer, Some of the different dimensions of prayer: Worship, Confession, Praying with the Bible, protection, intercession, requests, thanksgiving, listening, etc. Examples about the effectiveness of prayer in the Bible, in Church History, and today. This practical manual is like a "tool kit" that will help you enjoy your prayer time. Prayer is the greatest and noblest thing we can do for God and for man.

At the Heart of Prayer — Prayer in a group

This is a manual concerning prayer in the Church. It is a study of the book of Nehemiah with practical applications that relate to prayer in the Church: Preparation before action. Opposition. The source of revival. This book will help you deepen your personal prayer life and also prayer with others in the Church. This practical manual can be studied alone or in a group.

I Believe in prayer

Peter Maiden's recommendation concerning this book: "Ian Newberry has never ceased to challenge me in that most difficult area of my Christian life, my prayer life. This book not only gives that challenge but also offers real practical help in reviving your Church prayer meeting. It's biblical, it's extremely practical – A book not only to be read but to do!"

Thirty practical ideas to help you revive the prayer meeting. How to prepare the prayer meeting.

- How to motivate the participants.
- How to cultivate passion and compassion
- How to structure the prayer meeting
- How to intercede effectively: twenty-two different themes.
- How to develop a world vision

Available for God

Is fasting relevant to modern Christian living?

What are the physical benefits and dangers of going without food? What place has fasting held in Church history?

How does biblical fasting differ from fasting practised in other religions?

Available for God explores, from a biblical, medical and practical angle, why fasting is an important but neglected aspect of Christian spirituality. Biblical fasting means making ourselves completely available for God. This helpful volume will encourage you to think, pray and set time apart to be in God's presence and be fed by His Word.

Achevé d'imprimer en décembre 2017
sur les presses de l'imprimerie SEPEC
01960 Péronnas
pour le compte des Éditions Biblos

Imprimé en France
N° impression: N06962171114
Dépôt légal: décembre 2017